Twayne's United States Authors Series

Sylvia E. Bowman, *Editor*

INDIANA UNIVERSITY

John O'Hara

JOHN O'HARA

By SHELDON NORMAN GREBSTEIN

Harpur College, State University of New York

 103

CARNEGIE LIBRARY
LIVINGSTONE COLLEGE
SALISBURY, N. C. 28144

Twayne Publishers, Inc.   ::   New York

Copyright © 1966 by Twayne Publishers, Inc.

All Rights Reserved

Library of Congress Catalog Card Number: 66-17064

MANUFACTURED IN THE UNITED STATES OF AMERICA BY
UNITED PRINTING SERVICES, INC.
NEW HAVEN, CONN.

813.52
G799

73132

FOR
LARRY

Preface

DURING JOHN O'HARA'S long career he has published twenty-three volumes which have sold a total of some fifteen million copies. More important, we have now been reading O'Hara for thirty years. While it may be granted that a popular author need not be worthy of serious attention, and that a prolific author has no special claim upon us merely because he keeps busy, one who has held an inordinately fickle audience for more than a generation becomes indisputably an author to be reckoned with. He more than deserves our notice—he requires it.

The present study, therefore, has a dual purpose: it is at once an interpretation and an assessment. The reader of this first book-length study of O'Hara will soon discern that my admiration for O'Hara is considerable but not unqualified. While I have respect and affection for his writing, I do not wish to pass as a fanatical admirer of it; O'Hara's writing itself lacks that transcendent genius which inspires fanaticism. I also believe that O'Hara's cause is better served by careful analysis and balanced evaluation than by page after page of praise. In short, I have tried to fulfill one of the critic's primary functions: to distinguish the good from the bad in O'Hara's work so that his several excellences will be spared the blame rightly accruing to his defects. Above all, by means of a detailed consideration of O'Hara's technique, I have tried to illuminate some aspects of the operation of his exceedingly durable, expert talent. Few writers of the past half-century have achieved more with what they have, and many have achieved less with more.

O'Hara's career exhibits no single predominant development or shift which can be discerned as evolving consistently in time. However, since the very bulk of his writing makes some sort of grouping necessary, and since the major phases of his career lend themselves readily to a topical arrangement, I determined that a combined chronological and topical approach would most sensibly represent the patterns in O'Hara's work. Consequently, the book is ordered as follows:

Chapter One surveys O'Hara's critical reception over the past three decades, especially the reaction of the academic critics and literary historians. This chapter is also intended as an introduction to the issues and questions which have surrounded O'Hara's writing from the outset. Chapter Two offers in considerable detail a biographical sketch of the author's Pennsylvania boyhood: the experience which has provided him with the largest and most fertile source of raw material for his fiction. Chapter Three sets forth a book-by-book analysis of O'Hara's Pennsylvania fiction—including almost all of his major novels. Chapter Four is concerned with the other main body of his work, what I have called the New York-Hollywood phase. This chapter also includes pertinent biographical data. Chapter Five deals entirely with O'Hara's short fiction (elsewhere treated briefly in passing), concentrating on the themes and techniques recurring in his short-story collections. The final chapter ventures an estimate of O'Hara's attainments, concluding with the attempt to properly rank him among his contemporaries.

One of the chief pleasures and challenges in this task was the necessity for original interpretation. Almost all previous discussion of O'Hara has focused upon his gains and losses as a novelist of manners and as a social commentator; and, although no critical study of O'Hara could ignore these salient aspects of his work, the present study seeks to avoid reduplication by paying relatively less attention to them. I have made little conscious use of the opinions of others and have attempted, instead, to stress hitherto neglected characteristics of O'Hara's writing.

SHELDON NORMAN GREBSTEIN

Binghamton, New York
July 16, 1965

Acknowledgments

I wish to express my gratitude to the Research Foundation of the State University of New York for the award of both a Faculty Research Fellowship and Grant-in-Aid to assist me in the preparation of this book. I am also grateful to the Harpur Foundation for a grant covering the cost of manuscript typing.

My thanks to Miss Martha Covey, now with the Mobile, Alabama, Public Library, for her great help in the collection of materials. Likewise, my thanks to Mrs. Hazel Potts Leddy, of the Pottsville Free Public Library, and to Mr. Walter S. Farquhar, Miss Edith Patterson, and Mr. D. W. Davis of Pottsville for supplying me with valuable information.

I am sincerely grateful to my colleagues at Harpur College, Arthur Clements, Robert Kroetsch, Leonard Moss, John Hagopian, Derek Colville, and Glenn Burne, for reading the manuscript and offering cogent suggestions. Mr. Clements and Mr. Hagopian provided especially detailed and helpful advice.

A particular word of thanks to John K. Hutchens of Rye, New York, for his great kindness and generosity in several matters.

All quotations and excerpted material used herein fall under the "fair use" concept as it applies to critical and scholarly books. Separate acknowledgments of permission to quote are therefore omitted.

Contents

Chronology

1905   John Henry O'Hara born in Pottsville, Pennsylvania; the first of eight children of Dr. Patrick Henry O'Hara and Katherine Delaney O'Hara.

1911-   Boyhood in Pottsville; attended both public and parochial
1919   schools. Several summers spent with maternal grandparents in nearby Lykens, Pennsylvania. In his early teens sometimes acted as driver for his doctor-father during emergency calls.

1919-   Attended Keystone State Normal School and Fordham
1924   Preparatory School; dismissed from both. Graduated class valedictorian from Niagara Preparatory School, 1924. Began as reporter for Pottsville *Journal* later the same year.

1925   Accepted for admission to Yale; father's death prevented enrollment.

1926-   Continued to work as reporter for Pottsville *Journal* and
1927   Tamaqua (Pennsylvania) *Courier.*

1927-   After several months of travel and irregular employment,
1933   O'Hara came to New York City late 1927. Worked in various capacities as writer for New York *Daily Mirror, Morning Telegraph, Herald Tribune, Time* magazine, and Pittsburgh *Bulletin-Index.* Also employed as secretary to Heywood Broun, as public relations man, and as press agent for Warner Brothers. Discharged from most of these positions. Beginning in spring, 1928, published sketches and stories in the *New Yorker* and other magazines.

1931-   Married Helen Pettit, 1931; divorced, 1933.
1933

1934   *Appointment in Samarra* published; well received by both critics and public. O'Hara went to Hollywood as film writer, one of his chief occupations until the mid-1940's; residence alternated between New York and Hollywood.

1935   *The Doctor's Son and Other Stories* published. *Butter-field 8,* based on Starr Faithfull case, published; became great popular success.

1937   O'Hara married Belle Mulford Wylie, daughter of socially prominent physician.

1938   *Hope of Heaven* published. First of the "Pal Joey" stories published by the *New Yorker* in the fall.

1939   *Files on Parade* published.

1940   *Pal Joey* published. Adapted for the stage by O'Hara, with music and lyrics by Rodgers and Hart; had a successful Broadway run.

1940-
1942   O'Hara contributed "Entertainment Week" columns (reviews of current plays and movies) to *Newsweek.*

1944   Rejected for military service because of physical disability, O'Hara spent several months as war correspondent for *Liberty* magazine; assigned to Task Force 38 of Admiral Halsey's Third Fleet in the Pacific.

1945   Daughter, Wylie, born. *Pipe Night* published. O'Hara saddened by death of close friend Robert Benchley.

1947   *Hellbox* published.

1949   *A Rage to Live* published; enjoyed large sales despite mixed reviews. O'Hara had earlier moved to Princeton, New Jersey.

1951   *The Farmer's Hotel* published.

1952   *Pal Joey* successfully revived on Broadway; awarded Drama Critics' and Donaldson prizes as best musical play of 1952.

1953   O'Hara stricken by near-fatal hemorrhage resulting from stomach ulcers.

1954   January 9, O'Hara's wife Belle died of heart ailment at thirty-nine. O'Hara began bi-weekly "Appointment with O'Hara" columns for *Collier's;* continued until September, 1956. *Sweet and Sour* published.

1955   *Ten North Frederick* published; won favor of public and reviewers. Later given National Book Award in Fiction for 1955. O'Hara married Mrs. Katherine Barnes Bryan.

1956   *A Family Party* published.

1957   O'Hara elected to National Institute of Arts and Letters.

1958   *From the Terrace* published; large sales, majority of reviewers hostile.

1960   *Ourselves to Know* and *Sermons and Soda Water* published.

1961   *Five Plays* and *Assembly* published.

1962   O'Hara's mother died, age eighty-two. *The Big Laugh* and *The Cape Cod Lighter* published.

1963   *Elizabeth Appleton* published.

1964   *The Hat on the Bed* published. O'Hara received the American Academy of Arts and Letters Award of Merit, given every five years for notable achievement in the novel. *The Horse Knows the Way* published.

CHAPTER 1

O'Hara and the Critics

A SURVEY of the voluminous criticism of the work of John O'Hara during the past thirty years reveals three distinct, instructive, and essentially related facts: first, the bulk of this criticism consists of newspaper and periodical reviews of individual O'Hara works at the moment of their appearance; second, while reviews of O'Hara have probably been as often friendly as hostile, the adverse notices of O'Hara's books are remarkable for their vehemence and ferocity; third, considering the amount and variety of critical writing now done by academicians, surprisingly little of it has been directed to John O'Hara.

These facts lead unmistakably to the conclusion that O'Hara has not only been maligned but slighted. Certainly no other American fiction writer of comparable ability, achievement, and longevity has been treated with similar disdain by literary critics, scholars, and historians (as differentiated from reviewers). The refusal or unwillingness to deal with O'Hara must, therefore, be attributed largely to error or misunderstanding.

The injustice of O'Hara's "critical" fate stands out in even sharper relief when we contrast it to the academic fascination with someone like Salinger, an admittedly gifted writer but one whose accomplishment so far resides in only a single tantalizing short novel and in perhaps half a dozen first-rate stories. Even O'Hara's most hardened detractors would grant him that much achievement and more, yet The Establishment continues to busy itself with discussion about Salinger; for O'Hara, silence continues. To be statistical, Salinger was the subject for sixty-one separate items of criticism, including four books, during the past four years; O'Hara was the subject of two, one article and one monograph.[1] The situation causes one to wonder at the vagaries of critical taste and fashion.

If we also search in vain for close, detailed, and extensive treatments of O'Hara in the standard literary histories, we will at least find somewhat more cogent reasons for his omission or scant mention. Most of these histories were published before O'Hara's surge of productivity, beginning in 1955, demanded his reassessment. When the literary historian does deign to mention O'Hara, he tends to file the writer away neatly in a phrase, a line, a paragraph—rarely more—as a disciple of the Hemingway hard-boiled manner, as a follower of Fitzgerald, or as one of a particular species of modern and very minor Naturalist. For example, O'Hara is completely ignored in *The Literature of the American People* (1951); and, until its most recent edition, he was dismissed by the *Literary History of the United States* in a sentence and a phrase. In the sentence he is depicted as an analyst of "the mores of the emancipated speakeasy set"; in the phrase, he is lumped with James M. Cain and Raymond Chandler.[2]

While more recent literary surveys, chronicles, and histories tend to pay O'Hara slightly more attention, the appraisals continue to be either disproportionately brief or misleadingly facile. Thus the recent (1962), large, and generally admirable *Reader's Encyclopedia of American Literature* devotes half a column to O'Hara, which concludes as follows: "O'Hara is considered a master of the short story, an able commentator on a civilization he doesn't much care for, and an amusing portraitist of types not always particularly attractive."[3] The irritating aspect of this assessment is, however, that in the same compendious work Salinger, Marquand, and Dos Passos each receive from two to three times the space given O'Hara.

This reaction was undoubtedly influenced by the course of O'Hara's career during its first decade, for of his first three novels only *Appointment in Samarra* (1934) was of the type and quality to withstand hard scrutiny by studious observers. *Butterfield 8* (1935) had its merits, but its protagonist and its subject lacked appeal for the scholar-critic. *Hope of Heaven* (1938), a Hollywood novel, deserved oblivion because of its serious flaws. O'Hara's two collections of short stories during these years contained much work of very high quality, but they, too, somehow escaped notice, sharing in the indifference which greeted all but *Appointment in Samarra*. Thus by the early 1940's, despite the great merit of his first novel and his admirable accomplishments in the short-story form, including the *Pal Joey* sequence, O'Hara's reputation had been firmly nailed in place among the lower rungs on the ladder of literary prestige. His frequent concern with vivid but not very profound characters and situations of the Broadway-Hollywood world; the quiet, unspectacular manner of his short fiction; his association with the *New Yorker* magazine; his candid, even brutally frank treatment of sexuality; his lack of obvious commitment to a particular social or political standpoint—these and like factors combined to fix O'Hara in a predicament he has never quite surmounted.[4]

O'Hara also suffered from the effects of bad timing. He emerged at a moment in America when only strong political-social writing, especially that with proletarian leanings, could distract the most important critics from their bemusement over the literary splendors of the 1920's. One considers the applause which greeted Steinbeck, Dos Passos, Odets. Yet only *Appointment in Samarra* qualified for some of the same attention. One notes also that better artists than O'Hara endured the same neglect: Faulkner was unknown outside of a small coterie of devoted followers; Sinclair Lewis' enormous fame declined drastically; F. Scott Fitzgerald plummeted so swiftly and completely out of fashion that his most mature and resonant work, the agonizingly beautiful *Tender Is the Night,* caused barely a ripple of comment, when the homage it deserved might well have reinvigorated its shattered author and salvaged his career. Little wonder then that O'Hara, the writer of the new generation who most resembled Fitzgerald, failed to get due notice.

Much of what has been said should not, however, apply to the younger scholar-critics, presumably unconstrained by the tastes and prejudices of their elders. But O'Hara still awaits their attention. Where they have given it at all, it has been scornful and derisive. The scholastic label now usually applied to O'Hara is "hack."

Citations from two recent studies should illustrate the point. In his 1960 book *The Denatured Novel,* Albert Van Nostrand invokes O'Hara's work as an example of how the Hemingway influence has debauched popular fiction and also been corrupted by it. During his discussion Van Nostrand scores O'Hara for his essential hollowness of theme and characterization, for his duplicitous manipulation of ironic effects, for his repetitiveness of situation, and for his tedious detail. The critic concludes by denouncing even O'Hara's Realism as fakery.[5]

John W. Aldridge, who works himself up to even greater fury in his treatment of O'Hara, uses him as an object-lesson of the fate of writers who enjoy large audiences. According to Aldridge, O'Hara is one of the very few writers now at work who can satisfy the reader's demand for a *surface* reality which nevertheless allows his fantasy, especially his erotic fantasy, full play. Moreover, according to Aldridge, O'Hara satisfies his readers by reducing "the pursuit of the Good Life" to "the pursuit of the Good Lay"; by imitating the serious novel in his concern with the seamy side of life—although avoiding the serious novel's terrifying sense of truth; and by pandering to the reader's taste for pornography while at the same time sparing him from any deep and disturbing involvement in the writer's creation.[6]

After such vehemence from this generation's practicing critics, and even after taking into account better balanced and more restrained recent appraisals by John Portz, Russell Carson, and Jesse Bier,[7] it is a relief to turn to the reviewers who, whatever their judgment of O'Hara's worth, have at least given him continuing and often sympathetic attention. To be fair to the scholar-critics, it must be noted that many of the reviewers have been themselves members of the scholastic fraternity, who have for this occasion set aside their gowns and appear in public garb and in a public place. Among those who have at one time or another attended, as reviewers, to O'Hara's career are such distinguished academics as Lionel Trilling, R. P. Blackmur, Arthur Mizener, Irving Howe, and Alfred Kazin. They have not all spoken well of him, but at least they have spoken.

Accordingly, one finds in the New York *Times Book Review*, the New York *Herald Tribune Books*, the *Saturday Review*, the *Nation, New Republic, Atlantic, Time, Newsweek, New Yorker*, and others, a concern with O'Hara as persistent as the non-concern of the little magazines and scholarly journals. Herein there is a paradox. While the reviewers have been far from universally approving of O'Hara, while he has inspired as much vituperation as any prominent writer of the past thirty years, and while the reviewers have often concluded that O'Hara is really only a minor writer, the very range, frequency, and intensity of the reviews suggest the contrary. To put it simply, no minor nor merely popular writer could have either provoked or sustained such searching criticism; and one can only infer that, whatever his achievement, he has for his readers and critics a certain strong interest, a certain undeniable significance, a certain compelling and continuing attraction. Regardless of the nature of the reviewers' conclusions about O'Hara, they have awarded him the space, if not the close scrutiny, accorded only to a major writer; and in fact the question they almost inevitably ask about him (although it is rarely stated explicitly) is not whether he is worth reading, or why he is read, but whether he belongs among The Great. Opinion has been too divided to allow the formation of a firm and emphatic answer. Nevertheless, that the question has been asked constitutes praise of a high order.

What are the reviewers' reactions to O'Hara, as one surveys them over the years? First, there are the points in O'Hara's favor. Almost everyone agrees in almost every review that O'Hara has an unsurpassed acuity of vision for the insignia of social station, for the objects which fill or clutter our lives, and for the clothes, cars, houses, which comprise the surface and much of the texture of American life. Reviewers also concur that he hears American speech with such unparalleled accuracy and authenticity that his dialogue seems to have been recorded from life rather than written. One inspired reviewer summarized these faculties in the term "phono-photographic." Commingled with the praise of these virtues, and usually growing out of them, is the general respect for O'Hara as a social historian and social analyst: for his skill in depicting the tensions between classes, or between members of slightly different rank within the same class, or between one generation and another. That is, O'Hara wins commendation more for his insight into and manipulation of social insignia, customs, and mores than for his ability as a psychologist. Quite often, the reviewer predicts that future readers will return to O'Hara, not history books, to find out how it was to live in the first half of the twentieth century. Finally, many praise O'Hara as a stylist, especially in the short story; they approve of the terseness, clarity, and precision of his prose and of his professional deftness in making a story.

At this point the friendly critics begin to disagree. A minority finds O'Hara's depiction of sexuality (always a prominent matter in any O'Hara review) honest, appropriate, and not excessive. A minority finds him compassionate, engaged with and understanding of his fellow man. A minority asserts that he is really a moralist under the coldly objective surface of his work. As the reader may have surmised, I align myself with these minority views.

The bulk of the hostile criticism of O'Hara—especially as

directed to the long novels written between 1949 and 1960:
A Rage to Live, Ten North Frederick, From the Terrace, Ourselves to Know,—likewise rests upon several basic charges constantly reiterated. They are: (1) O'Hara is at best a superb reporter who raises journalism to an extraordinarily high level but falls short as an artist because he subordinates theme, character, and action to a massive verisimilitude in physical detail. (2) His objectivity is either a disguise for his mindlessness or the expression of his essential callousness and moral indifference. (3) He writes clearly but also flatly and transparently. (4) Obsessed with the bedroom antics of his characters, O'Hara regales the reader endlessly and pointlessly with them. (5) He has failed to develop; his first work, *Appointment in Samarra,* remains his best. (6) His portrayal of the rich, often vivid but unconvincing, is chiefly significant for its reflection of the writer's enmity toward his imagined people. (7) He is little more than a skillful hack whose main motivation for writing, and for writing so much, is lust for gold.

Unfortunately, one who has read both O'Hara's work itself with the utmost concentration and then scrutinized the criticism levied upon it does not come away persuaded that the critics have entirely fulfilled their responsibility to O'Hara—and least of all the academic critics. Rather, it appears that much which has been written about O'Hara depends upon a casual, cursory, and even slipshod reading of him. Critics have too often read him as one reads an entertainer, not as one reads an author whose very survival during more than a generation of shifting literary taste, whose very productivity, whose hold upon a large and loyal audience, whose depiction of certain crucial segments of our life and times, and whose power to win distinguished adherents to his cause, all demand that he be given consideration as a serious artist, possibly as a serious artist of major stature. Not having read him closely, the very subtlety of his effects and the very saliency of his insights have escaped them. Not having read him closely, they have missed much of the best that is in him.

CHAPTER 2

The Pennsylvania Years

A S ONE COUNTS years alone, most of John O'Hara's life has been lived away from Pottsville, Pennsylvania, the place of his birth; since in 1927, at the age of twenty-two, O'Hara left Pottsville, never to return as a resident and only infrequently as a visitor. But a life is comprised of more than the sum of its years, and a writer's life expresses itself not in the names of places and in the time spent in them, but in the imaginative re-creation of those places and the remembrance of what was there experienced. In the artistic process of re-creation and remembrance geography becomes inscape: streets, houses, people, are transmuted from a physical into a psychical reality; events submit to a reordering and a retelling; relationships are perceived where the record may contain no "proof" they ever existed; and what was only fact becomes Truth.

By this means many of our best writers have transformed the mundane actuality of their shaping environments into other, more permanent forms: Hemingway's Michigan, Paris, Italy, Spain; Faulkner's Mississippi; Steinbeck's California; Lewis' Minnesota; Anderson's Ohio; Wolfe's North Carolina. To this list O'Hara's Pennsylvania bids addition; for in a series of memorable novels and short stories O'Hara has also created a country of his own, a country existing both in the form of an actual terrain, with cities and people, and as an imaginative design within the pages of a fiction. Despite his wanderings and his later residence in Hollywood, New York, and, since 1949, in Princeton, New Jersey, it is to the Pennsylvania of his youth that O'Hara has returned most often for the locale and for much of the subject matter of his best work.

Pottsville, the "Gibbsville" of O'Hara's fiction, is located in northeastern Pennsylvania in the heart of the anthracite coal region. If one were to use Harrisburg ("Fort Penn" in *A Rage to Live*) and Philadelphia as the base for a slightly askew triangle to be drawn on a map, Pottsville would lie near the figure's apex. Just to the northeast of Pottsville is Tamaqua, where O'Hara was "farmed out" as a young newspaperman, after having performed less than satisfactorily for the Pottsville *Journal*. To the west is Lykens, the "Lyons" of *Ourselves to Know*, where as a lad O'Hara spent happy summers with his maternal grandparents.[1] The "Port Johnson" of Alfred Eaton's boyhood in *From the Terrace* probably also lies within a hundred miles of Pottsville, either as a real town or as a composite. This area comprises what O'Hara's readers have come to recognize as O'Hara's special domain; they call it "the O'Hara country."

A stranger visiting Pottsville today might persuade himself, without a too-forbidding sense of his own recklessness, that he can visualize the town as it must have been in 1905, when O'Hara was born, and as it must have been in the 'teens and early 1920's, during O'Hara's boyhood and adolescence. Although the downtown streets bustle with shoppers and although one sees here and there a new building in Pottsville's center, as well as the usual suburban developments, the town manifests a sense of age, changelessness, longevity, even decay. Pottsville is not pretty. The railroad tracks parallel Main Street and are separated from it by only one block. Most of the houses are wood, two or three stories high, crowded closely together, many of them fronting directly on the steep, narrow streets. That Pottsville's economic base has always been primarily industrial may be inferred from the shops, warehouses, smoke-stained housefronts; that coal was once king there is evident in the slashed hillsides, mounds of rubble, and huge scrap piles of rusted equipment which deface the surrounding countryside. Withal, Pottsville retains an unmistakable dignity and character. Its older residents speak of it with pride and possessiveness. Despite its ungainliness, it is no more unsightly than many other small industrial cities of the Northeast, and it is infinitely more attractive than comparable communities in Pennsylvania and West Virginia.

Mahantonga Street, the "Latenengo Street" which to O'Hara's characters signifies wealth and respectability, still is recognized as among Pottsville's most desirable addresses. The lower end of Mahantonga close to Main Street consists largely of offices occupied by doctors and lawyers; O'Hara himself was born at Second and Mahantonga streets, also the site of his father's office. Later, the family moved to a house at Sixth and Mahantonga, undoubtedly something of an improvement since Mahantonga Street becomes more imposing as it climbs.[2] Most of the structures in the area, narrow houses of brick, are now shabby, even decrepit; but one sees in them and in the occasional remaining huge and ornate house a vestige of the town's wealth during its coal and iron days, the days of O'Hara's boyhood.[3]

John O'Hara was the oldest of eight children born to Dr. Patrick Henry O'Hara and his wife Katherine. Dr. O'Hara came to Pottsville after his medical training, when he was appointed by the Directors of the Poor of Schuylkill County as superintendent of the county's hospital facilities for the poor and of the insane asylum.[4] Later, he became the first resident physician of the Pottsville Hospital and established a reputation as one of the town's most capable and dedicated physicians.

In a memoir written twenty-five years after his father's death, O'Hara said with pride: "My father was the leading surgeon in a part of the world where good surgeons are not rare. He was a great doctor. He could get out of bed at two in the morning and tell me to get out of bed and help him hitch the horse to a sleigh, and drive to the hospital. That one I remember especially. A runaway train wreck, and I, a kid of maybe twelve, had to hold the hand of one man who was dying of burns and another who was dying after amputation of both legs. These men just wanted to have a hand to hold on the way out. The nurses were busy." In the same piece O'Hara also wrote: "I remember that one night when he was in white tie and tails, on his way to a medical club dinner, he crawled under a trolley car to free a newsboy who had been run over by the car."[5]

O'Hara's father seems to have been an unusual man in other ways. From the glimpses of him (portrayed as "Dr. Malloy") one gets in O'Hara's novels and stories, and from what one gleans in the reminiscences of Pottsvillians, he was a vibrant, hearty man who loved sports, dressed with impeccable taste, expressed his opinions with candor and bluntness, rigidly abstained from spirits and tobacco, avowed a strict code of conduct which he expected others to follow, and yet possessed a lively sense of humor and keen sensitivity. It is amusing that two old-time residents of Pottsville remember Dr. O'Hara in almost identical terms. One calls him a "splendid, polished gentleman" but "another one of your hot-tempered Irishmen if he took a dislike to you."[6] The other describes him as "an immaculate, polished gentleman," with a little dark mustache and a husky, vigorous physique. "He was always lively and joking, but he'd give you a crack in the jaw if you came at him the wrong way," the second concludes, with a mixture of awe and fondness.[7] From this evidence, one can locate a source for the now-legendary temper of O'Hara the writer.

O'Hara's mother, Katherine Delaney O'Hara, whose parents were people of substance, was also a far from ordinary person. Once again such phrases as "polished, well-educated woman" and "very refined lady" occur in the accounts of Pottsville's citizens who knew the O'Hara family.[8] She had a gift for mimicry which one researcher into O'Hara's background has speculated may have influenced her son's sensitivity to the spoken word.[9] Unusually well-educated for a woman of her generation, Mrs. O'Hara could speak French and play bridge in a time and place where such abilities were not common.[10] Doubtless she had a crucial part in the development of O'Hara's acute interest in manners.

There is scant evidence that O'Hara suffered from the same kind of traumatic experience during boyhood as that endured by Dreiser or Sinclair Lewis. The O'Hara family was large but, from all available evidence, tightly knit and compatible. Those who knew the parents remember their marriage as one completely free from rumors of dissension or scandal. All the children appear to have enjoyed good health, good enough to have survived to this date. Moreover, despite the family's size, while Dr. O'Hara lived they enjoyed considerable prosperity. O'Hara himself has been at pains to point out that the legend of his being a poor boy from the wrong side of the tracks lacks all foundation in fact. Among the family's possessions, he avows, were five automobiles owned simultaneously; a farm of one hundred and sixty acres; and livestock which included a bull of high lineage, various mules, horses, ponies, and his own personal five-gaited mare. He recalls that his parents belonged to a number of the best clubs, shopped at fashionable Philadelphia stores, and sent him to private tutors and dancing classes.[11] Accounts by Pottsvillians corroborate O'Hara's statements. One remembers the O'Haras as a solid, "conservative" family. Another says, "The O'Haras travelled with a crowd not downtrodden by any means; professional people and not all Irish."

Nor was there any powerful emotional deprivation. O'Hara was a high-spirited youth given to such pranks as the assault (with another boy) on the headquarters of the local German-American club because they had convinced themselves it was being used for espionage activities. His independence and stubbornness undoubtedly often put him at sword's point with his father, and these characteristics on one occasion led to his overnight incarceration in the town jail.[12] There may also have been some conflict with his father over his choice of occupation, as is evidenced by a passage from "The Doctor's Son," an early autobiographical story. The speaker is Dr. Malloy, and the instance concerns a massive influenza epidemic which demands that the physicians behave as heroes: "To think that a son of mine would rather rot in a dirty, stinking newspaper office than do this. Why, I do more good and make more money in twenty minutes in the operating room than you'll be able to make the first three years you're out of college. If you go to college." However, as one learns in the same story and in another early, autobiographical story "It Must Been Spring," there was a deep and abiding love between father and son strong enough to annul all disagreements and conflicts.[13]

O'Hara grew to young manhood seemingly without suffering any of the handicaps of the tormented and rejected child who later projects, expiates, or transubstantiates his early agonies into art: a Poe, a Dickens, a Kafka. Indeed, the researcher into O'Hara's past turns up a story of a bumptious, irrepressible, and no doubt at times insufferable youth. At seventeen he was, in his own words, a "rounder," and an "unpredictable, rather offensive young squirt."[14] Dismissed from two schools, Fordham Prep and Keystone State Normal, for various infractions, O'Hara finally finished his secondary education at Niagara Prep, graduating as class valedictorian with grades of "97" in English and "88" in Spanish.[15] According to one account, even that glorious occasion was dimmed when Dr. O'Hara apprehended his son coming in at seven o'clock in the morning after an all-night celebration, and thereupon determined that, before John went to college, he would first have a further taste of the strenuous life.[16]

However, although O'Hara was thought by some to be "independent," "cocky," "fresh," and "sarcastic," others knew a different phase of his temperament. "John was well-liked, but he was pretty much a loner," a boyhood friend recalled. "You could never get too close to him." They describe him as reserved and endlessly curious. One contemporary remembers, "As a kid, he used to sit by the tracks and watch the freights go by. When he grew up, he could tell you the name of every railroad in the United States. The same thing applied to horses, Christian creeds, cars, music, and just about everything."[17]

Undoubtedly this sensitive and inquisitive nature, disguised under the brash and exuberant exterior, later manifested itself in the writer. Sometime during his youth the nuances of social position and class structure also invited, or were forced upon, his attention. As his own *Appointment in Samarra* makes abundantly clear, an Irish Catholic might gain access to the town's polite society; but there was a point beyond which he might not go. Perhaps, with the Depression, this barrier dissolved under the impact of social upheaval; yet it had been true, or more important, O'Hara *believed* it to be true during his own youth. The lesson was dramatized when O'Hara fell in love with a girl from one of the town's most eminent families but, discouraged from pursuing the romance, was embittered against the entire set to which the family belonged. One Pottsvillian remembers this group as "very prudish" and "stiff-necked"—to the degree that if a young man at a social affair were seen too much in the vicinity of the punchbowl, he became the subject of gossip. Moreover, another long-time resident of Pottsville has remarked that the community's socially élite represented the Philadelphia influence and its concomitant ethnic and religious strains rather than the Irish or Pennsylvania German elements more typical of the locality. This resident also recalls that there was "at least a friendship" between O'Hara and a girl from an old, rich Pottsville family.[18]

Thus, although O'Hara might have been somewhat oversensitive about his social status, there appears to be a factual basis for an extremely revealing passage which appears in *Butterfield 8,* and is spoken by O'Hara's fictional alter ego, the young newspaperman Jimmy Malloy. Malloy states bitterly that, despite his correct clothing and manners and horsemanship, his identity as a "Mick" forever catalogues him and bars him from high society. "I'm pretty God damn American, and therefore my brothers and my sisters are, and yet we're not American. We're Micks, we're non-assimilable, we Micks."[19] The prejudice among Pottsville's élite against the Irish—a prejudice apparently still very active during O'Hara's youth—derived in part from the town's experience with the "Molly Maguires," a secret society of insurgents who became involved in the conflict between labor and management in the Pennsylvania anthracite coal region during the 1860's and 1870's and who resorted to terrorist methods, including murder, to gain their ends. Doubtless the activities of the Molly Maguires against the coal and iron interests (from which many wealthy Pottsvillians drew their fortunes) continued to militate against the social aspirations of anyone of Irish origin, long after the society was disbanded and the last of its activists punished.[20]

Together with this sense of social alienation that was later to stimulate some of the keenest passages of his fiction, O'Hara's early newspaper work was also producing its effect on him. Quite apart from any influence journalism might have had on his literary style, it confronted him with a mass of stark, basic experience from which he derived the hard-boiled attitude characteristic of much of his early writing. The recent story "In the Silence" contains this illuminating piece of self-analysis, offered by the now middle-aged Malloy as a reflection upon his own youth:

> A young newspaper reporter sees so much in the first few years that he begins to think he's seen it all. That makes for a very unattractive wise-guy attitude, what I call unearned cynicism. After you've lived a good many years I don't see how you can be anything but cynical, since all any of us have a right to expect is an even break, and not many get that. But I thought I knew it all, and I didn't. It took me many more years to realize that a reporter covering general news lives an abnormal life, in that he sees people every day at the highest or lowest point of their lives. Day after day after day, people in trouble with the law, having accidents, losing control of themselves—or experiencing great successes. In one month's time a district man would see enough crime and horror and selfishness to last most people the rest of their lives.[21]

Furthermore, although O'Hara's career as a newspaperman was not conspicuous for its success either in Pottsville or later in New York, doubtless the necessity to write constantly, to get the facts down quickly, to avoid rhetorical self-indulgence, to concentrate on factual detail, to keep his eyes and ears open wide, were valuable to him, as newspaper experience has been for many an American writer.[22] Significant, also, is O'Hara's statement in a column which he wrote for the Pottsville *Journal* of May 2, 1925, that he intended some day to write "the Great American Novel."

However, of all O'Hara's experiences as a young man the one which affected him most profoundly was the sudden death of his father in 1925. Although Dr. O'Hara was sixty at the time of his death, he had been so vigorous a man and so much the mainstay of his family that his loss was doubly appalling. As O'Hara later wrote, his father died from overwork, just one week after his return from a Florida vacation taken to restore his health: "He came home to die. . . . He had a funeral almost as big as a gangster's or a politician's and he left no money to speak of. But the people who turned up at the church—the Protestants and Jews as well as the Catholics—were not there only for the spectacle."[23]

Dr. O'Hara's death had two important effects. First, it drastically altered the condition of the family's financial status and its plans for the future. Dr. O'Hara had made unwise investments by speculating heavily in German marks in the belief they would regain their pre-war value; and, although the family was able to maintain appearances for a while through the sale of some bonds that Mrs. O'Hara held, its situation was precarious. The family had gone "from professional-class security to near poverty almost literally overnight."[24] Under these circumstances there was no chance that John, the eldest son, could fulfill his ambition of enrolling at Yale, which had already accepted him. The disappointment was undeniably severe and certainly influenced his later life, but a recent profile of O'Hara in *Newsweek* rightly warns against the error in assuming simplistically, as many critics have over the years, that all of O'Hara's interest in social distinctions, clubs, and college background is a compensation for his own failure to attend college.

This rather neat explanation of an entire phase of a writer's career probably has been kept alive by the famous anecdote, originally related in print by O'Hara himself. In this episode Hemingway was supposed to have suggested to his traveling companions Vincent Sheean and John Lardner that they use some surplus monies to begin a fund to send O'Hara to Yale.[25] However, as O'Hara told an interviewer in 1960: "I wanted desperately to go to Yale, and it was a terrible shock and disappointment when I found I couldn't go. But this was thirty-five years ago and it is simply not true that I've been brooding about it ever since."[26]

More important, his father's death stimulated, as it inevitably does in any young person who buries a beloved parent, hard thoughts about life, death, and the meaning of man's existence. Walter Farquhar, who knew O'Hara well at the time, has written: "A thinker to begin with, John was obliged to do some deep thinking during the period of frustration following his father's death. Proud and sensitive, he felt keenly his inability to aid his family immediately. It was then he became a satirist in the fashion of Petronius. It was then he began to look with bitterness upon the mores of his times."[27]

Sometime also during the years surrounding his father's decease and beginning in his late teens, O'Hara abandoned the Roman Catholicism which he had devoutly practiced as a boy and turned away completely from formal religion; one does not find any extensive or thorough discussion of religion in his work.[28] Religion usually appears only as part of the characterization of the Irish servants who play minor roles in O'Hara's Pennsylvania novels. Perhaps the most revealing remark about religion occurs in *Sermons and Soda Water,* when Jim Malloy (now in his early thirties) tells a girl with whom he is emotionally involved: "It's gone from me, Julie. The priests have ruined it for me."[29]

The death of Dr. O'Hara intensified and culminated the changes working upon O'Hara in Pottsville, and one becomes increasingly tempted to view the unhappy end of O'Hara's youth as the beginning of his pervasive pessimism. As this study later attempts to demonstrate, O'Hara never completely yields to it nor does he forbid his characters free will. Nevertheless, we see throughout his work the operation of an unpredictable and often overwhelming fate. It may be a fate dependent upon a character flaw; it may arise from the pressure of circumstances; it may result from an apparently casual act or decision; or it may simply be external—an act of nature or pure chance. But, in any case, his fiction makes recurrent use of situations in which lives proceed along well-ordered and planned avenues only to smash against totally unforeseen obstacles.

How like an abstraction of the author's own experience this disaster seems: a large, happy family enjoys a prosperous standard of living provided by its head, one of the city's more respected and successful men; the oldest son is on his way to Yale; then, the father dies and all the family's plans collapse together with its life-style. One might well emerge from such an experience with fatalism, suspicion toward life, awareness of the grinning skull under the smiling flesh, and the belief that "all any of us have a right to expect is an even break, and not many get that."[30]

Not long after his father's death O'Hara left home for larger, more cosmopolitan places; but in what might be called the second half of his career, that beginning in 1949 with *A Rage to Live,* Pennsylvania people and locales have been involved in five of the six novels published in the last fifteen years, playing their part also in his impressive output of *novellas* and short stories. The significance of his Pennsylvania youth has not been better described than in O'Hara's own words. In this moving, autobiographical passage from *Sermons and Soda Water,* O'Hara writes:

> After I became reconciled to middle age and the quieter life I made another discovery: that the sweetness of my early youth was a persistent and enduring thing, so long as I kept it at a distance of years. Moments would come back to me, of love and excitement and music and laughter that filled my breast as they had thirty years earlier. It was not nostalgia, which only means homesickness, nor was it a wish to be living that excitement again. It was a splendid contentment with the knowledge that once I had felt those things . . . deeply and well. . . . I wanted none of it ever again, but all I had I wanted to keep. . . . They were the things I knew before we knew everything, and, I suppose, before we began to learn. . . . In middle age I was proud to have lived according to my emotions at the right time, and content to live that way vicariously and at a distance. I had missed almost nothing, escaped very little, and at fifty I had begun to devote my energy and time to the last, simple but big task of putting it all down as well as I knew how.[31]

No other body of experience, despite the great quantity and variety of it O'Hara was later to know, has ever served him and his readers so well.

CHAPTER 3

Love, Failure, and Death in
the O'Hara Country

ALTHOUGH O'HARA'S CAREER has been in such constant flux that one finds it extremely difficult to hit upon simple but accurate categories, an important general truth does declare itself: that the bulk of O'Hara's work falls into two divisions, each of which contains roughly half of his total publication: (1) the writing which concerns itself with the lives of men and women set in the O'Hara country, Pennsylvania; (2) the writing which treats the lives of men and women as they are differently lived in the vicinities of Broadway and Hollywood. Within these broad categories, another distinction can be made. O'Hara is most consistently at his best (one is tempted to say O'Hara is "more at home") in those fictions employing the Pennsylvania setting; for, despite the cleverness, skill, and humor which he brings to his Broadway-Hollywood material, he has made of it nothing to equal the Pennsylvania stories.

These statements could be interpreted to mean that O'Hara is merely a regionalist, a modern counterpart of Kirkland, Howe, and Garland. Not so. O'Hara's people, not the places, are what endure in the memory. Gibbsville, Fort Penn, Lyons, Port Johnson, and Spring Valley are significant far less in themselves than as the homes for O'Hara's characters. Of course, the culture, institutions, class structure, and mores of these towns bear heavily upon O'Hara's work, often demanding the reader's closest attention, but when O'Hara functions at his best—when he functions as a novelist rather than as a historian—the setting becomes subordinated to the humans who inhabit it; it takes its vitality from them. The O'Hara country becomes real only as he succeeds in dramatizing milieu as the arena for human experience, as the context for his studies of love and death. "Gibbsville is my Yoknapatawpha County," he told an interviewer in 1955. "The physical design is that of Pottsville, as it exists. . . . But what it amounts to is that I've taken a real town and made it conform to a novelist's idea."[1]

I Appointment in Samarra:
Forces, Free Will, and Self-Knowledge

The tragedies of our time are very likely to be what Arthur Miller has called the tragedy of the common man. These are the tragedies of the mundane, the ordinary, the familiar: tragedies of men worn down by the everyday pressures of life or by their own inner pressures; pressures of earning bread; finding and maintaining an identity; of doing useful work; of keeping the love of one's wife, children, neighbors; of expressing one's simple human dignity; of remaining decent in the concrete jungle, the social jungle, the factory jungle, or the army jungle. So the tragedy of Julian English, of Gibbsville, Pennsylvania, who expires in his own garage during the evening of the day after Christmas, 1930, is a tragedy of the common man, a tragedy of the surrender to these attritive forces. It is, indeed, doubly a tragedy of the common man; for Julian's motivation for suicide derives partly from the belated discovery of his own commonness, of the terrifying recognition of his own susceptibility to the failures, pains, and defeats others had earlier confronted. The trials and disappointments which early come to ordinary men presented themselves to Julian during three packed days of a Christmas holiday; and he was not capable of absorbing the lesson. A few hours before Julian kills himself, he falls into a drunken sleep "wishing he knew more things," but it is too late for him to learn.[2]

Appointment in Samarra thus seems to chronicle the unhappy history of a man wholly victimized by Forces, especially Fate and Society. Fate appears to operate through the compulsion which drives Julian to throw a drink into Harry Reilly's face, the event which begins the protagonist's swift slide to doom. Fate is presumably the theme of the novel's epigraph, which retells the ancient tale of man who seeks to flee death only to find that in his very flight he keeps his destined appointment with it. Fate is also suggested in Caroline English's agonized reflection after her husband's death that "It was *time* for him to die" (294).

Society, too, takes a significant part in Julian's history. As one recent commentator has interpreted the novel, "... place is agency, and the tragedy depends upon the disguised impetus of the sociological forces."[3] Another critic states: "What makes *Appointment in Samarra* remarkable ... is not the story of Julian English; it is the story of Gibbsville. All the characters, even Julian English, are here for not their own sakes but because they represent significant social elements in Gibbsville...."[4]

Certainly these observations are pertinent, and no understanding of the novel would be complete without the recognition of the influence of Fate and Society upon the book's characters and action. Social status occupies an especially prominent position in the minds of O'Hara's fictional people; accordingly, much detail is given to family background, wealth, clothing—even to the social meaning of such seeming trivialities as the price of the various entrées on the country club's dinner menu. True, there exists in Gibbsville a delicate relationship between the various classes, religions, and ethnic groups. True, there is much snobbery both petty and vicious, notably the prejudices against Jews and Catholics. True, in Gibbsville one begins at birth with particular advantages and disadvantages. True, finally, O'Hara depicts all this with such convincing thoroughness and admirable subtlety that *Appointment in Samarra* would be a far weaker book without it.

But to his cognizance of these forces the sensitive reader must add a third element, one I believe to be crucial: free will. As I interpret the novel, Julian's tragedy derives less from fate, less from social pressure, than from a series of wrong choices, bungled acts, and misinterpretations which reflect his immaturity and defective character. He behaves as he is—a man who does not know himself. If a fatalism does operate, it is neither an occult power nor an exterior force but a fatalism in the way men are, of human nature. The tragedy, therefore, depends not so much upon circumstance but upon the failure of love, nerve, will. Or, to put it in another way, the tragedy could have been averted at almost any stage by the exercise of love, nerve, will. Even Julian's apparently uncontrollable impulse to attack Harry Reilly can be seen, like his other compulsions, as the outlet for an accumulation of past emotions. His impulses are, in fact, but one aspect of a destructiveness symptomatic of a life deficient in love, trust, and moral value. By the same token, as I will later argue, Julian's tragedy amounts to something more than a treatise about an individual who violates group protocols or an illustration of the rigidity of class structure in a small Pennsylvania city.

What, then, is the emotional history of Julian English; upon what foundations does his character at thirty stand? Most important—and this is a dominant and recurrent theme in O'Hara's fiction—is the failure of love between parents and children and, more specifically, between father and son. Because of one boyhood mistake, some petty larceny performed partly as a boyish prank and partly as a means for Julian to assert his place in the gang, Dr. English comes to think of his son as a thief and a weakling. The father's judgment, reinforced by his undemonstrative nature and by his stern, unbending righteousness, forever bends the twig of Julian's personality. To protect his own ego, already threatened by his own father's reputation as an embezzler and a suicide, Dr. English dissociates himself from his son at exactly the moment when Julian most needs assurance of his love. The father of another boy involved in the same escapade handles the matter with greater compassion. He severely punishes his son but continues to favor him. In contrast, by detaching himself from his son and his son's mistakes Dr. English cuts Julian adrift in a world without god, a world without authority, meaning, and hope of redemption; for to a boy god is manifested in his father.

This crucial rejection has several results, some of them ambivalent, as they often are in people. For one, Julian reacts against his father and all his father represents: a profession, an ordered life, respectability, restraint, politeness. Only to *Father* Creedon, Julian's father-surrogate, can he admit that he should have become a doctor. In his rebellion he releases his pent-up anger, the need to hit back and hurt and destroy, wishing subconsciously that he will be caught and punished.[5] At the same time Julian wants to be liked, admired, accepted: to have from others what he cannot have from his father. He develops a charm which is enhanced by his good looks and supported by the family's prosperity, charm which he can exercise on those higher social levels of Gibbsville automatically open to him through the English name, money, and Aryan background. Accordingly, Julian becomes a "personality," but one without an identity; for in O'Hara's world the boy also first learns his identity from his father. Julian's mother might have compensated for the father's failure, as the mother sometimes does in O'Hara's fiction, but we are told nothing about her except that she is a sweet, adoring woman, obviously without the strength or influence to fill the role of both parents.

Because Julian never fully assumes a stable identity, he can never grow up. He can never perform the adult function of understanding himself in relation to others; his own emotions remain of prime importance to him. All these sins of omission and commission return to torment him in the frantic days before his death. He has made few loyal friends to stand by him in his crisis. Rather, his country-club associates step back to see how well he can sail out the tempest he has himself blown up. Instead of appealing for help to the one person who could have been his salvation, his wife Caroline, he alienates her by making her the target for his anger and frustration. For a time a saving rapport is almost established, but at the club dance on the night following the Reilly episode—a dance they have come to in a mood of intimacy—he ignores her a little too long and violates her tender feeling. Then, rebuked, like the child he is, he takes revenge by humiliating her in public for what he has suffered in private.

Later, on the afternoon of the day culminating in his suicide, he says to Caroline: "This is a pretty good time for you to stick by me. . . . Blind, without knowing, you could stick by me. That's what you'd do if you were a real wife. . . ." As much as Julian needs such unquestioning loyalty and love—as much as he needed it from his father and, failing to get it there, goes on needing it from everyone else—Julian does not deserve what he demands. Even if given it, he would probably not repay it. And the final choice remains his. To gain Caroline's support, he has only to remain with her and tell her what troubles him; but arrogantly and pettishly he refuses, flaunting her warning: "Julian, if you leave now it's for good. Forever" (256). Thus the second support for Julian's life, his beautiful wife in whom he takes pride, is lost, this time largely by his own action.

Yet another of the pillars shoring up his existence is demolished when Froggy Ogden tells Julian he has never liked him, a crucial admission to a man who had needed to think of himself as popular and well-liked because inwardly he had feared the contrary. And at this phase in the discussion of the protagonist, one must take into account the social realities of Gibbsville as they impinge upon character and behavior.

Of first importance is the fact that Gibbsville society is not a steel trap which, once sprung, relentlessly holds its victim. Rather, it is a shifting, fluid society, a society in transition in which old and rigid lines are being dissolved under the multiple impact of emergent elements in the town's population and the exigencies of the Depression. To note but two examples of this change, there is the upward mobility of Harry Reilly, the Irish Catholic with his crude manners and smutty stories, who pushes his way toward the top because he is tough, clever, and strong. Similarly, the lawyers of Polish background who are Julian's antagonists at the Gibbsville Club have made their way into this once-exclusive establishment because they are now too able and prominent to be suppressed. Even the Jews at the bottom of the Gibbsville scale have begun to climb, first to residence on Latenengo Street, and soon, one infers, to club membership—just as the Poles and the Irish have already made it.

Nor does Julian's conduct immediately cost him his social place. When Julian loses control with Reilly, his friends back away warily, but they neither turn upon him nor against him. He is not suspended from the club, not reprimanded, not even cold-shouldered; their final attitude and conduct toward him will depend upon his future behavior, just as other club members have acted foolishly in the past without suffering drastic punishment. Further, Julian's behavior looms much more horrendously in his own mind than in anyone else's. As O'Hara shows us at the end of the novel, Harry Reilly continues to think of Julian as a gentleman and to be proud that Julian likes him—despite Julian's humiliation of him. Froggy Ogden, despite his avowed dislike for Julian and his insults, takes his side against the Polish lawyers in the fist-fight (completely confounding Julian's antagonists). Father Creedon, spokesman for the Catholic community, offers him comfort. Lute Fliegler, representative of the middle class and of the strong Pennsylvania-Dutch element, continues to be Julian's friend and advisor. Ed Charney and Al Grecco, the bootleggers O'Hara uses to represent Gibbsville's lower class and *demimonde*, do not condemn Julian for the episode with the roadhouse entertainer; time and an apology would have squared Julian with them also.

Of course, Julian's outrageous behavior will have social consequences. But in *Appointment in Samarra* society is neither the god nor the unknowable, juggernaut force that the plurality of critics have described. It has its stupidities, its cruelties, its excrescences; but it depends largely upon basic human needs and upon the observation of fundamental decencies. It sets forth only one strong rule that a violator breaks at his great hazard; one must not publicly offend the dignity of others, and even when this does occur, the transgressor can find ways to restore himself to good standing. Thus it is less a problem of "society" than of the verities of human nature, of the ego. Some of Gibbsville's citizens may have an exaggerated sense of what that dignity means; but, although these may be the "best people," they are rarely the most admirable human beings. Dr. English is perhaps the prime example of this self-assumed superiority, and his snobbery is a function of his own inadequacies and anxieties.

Having remarked these social realities, we may return now to complete the inquiry into the novel's central character. Two final aspects of Julian's emotional history remain to be explored: the influences of sex and money, powerful determinants in O'Hara's work.

Learning that Froggy Ogden and perhaps others have always disliked him is the second great discovery in Julian's life. Had he lived, this discovery might have brought about a change in him toward the better—toward humility. His first great discovery, however, had been that of his own sexual power: his ability to control his physical passion so as to be able to give his sexual partner prolonged pleasure. (Doubtless it was O'Hara's daring in broaching such facts of human behavior which offended the early critics and which has continued to offend others.) While O'Hara does not explore all the ramifications of the subject, the reader arrives at the sure conclusion that Julian's discovery of his special ability had been essential to his jauntiness and self-assurance. With that power over women, he could think himself very much a man, at least in one basic sense; and the conviction of his own masculinity had produced the peculiar charm and insouciance which springs from a man's total self-confidence with women. It had attuned him to women as sexual creatures, leading him to the belief that he could have anyone he wanted and keep her as long as he wanted. Nor does O'Hara minimize this factor. As his work demonstrates again and again, his men and women are sexual creatures; and the men are especially subject to the urges of their sexual needs.

To O'Hara's credit, he does not let the issue drop just there; he has more respect for humans than to portray them as laboratory specimens reacting only to physical stimuli. As Julian learns to his chagrin—both with his own wife and then, just before his death, with the reporter Alice Cartwright—a self-respecting woman has her values and her times of strength which make her proof against the most accomplished lover. She insists upon recognition as a person, as an entity. Julian begins to realize this fact during the final three days of his life when he reflects that his physical intimacy with his wife has not also given him possession of her soul (35-36). Unfortunately, Julian fails to act upon this realization; nor is there evidence that he tries. He has too long depended upon charm and his body to begin to treat his wife, or any attractive woman, with full human decency. Ultimately, Julian's sexual power turns against him. It has given him one kind of perception at the expense of another, more important kind. His blindness costs him the only two women he ever loves: the Polish girl, Mary, who Julian realizes sometime during the drunken haze of the last few hours of his life, had also loved him; and the other, the fatal loss, his wife.

Just as the shallowness of Julian's sexual values assist in his crucial self-deception, so does his inability to manage money, to take it seriously, to understand its meaning (the same character flaw in another manifestation) mark a further milestone on the way to his collapse. Product of a boom time and a wealthy home, graduate of a college but possessor of no durable knowledge, skill, or talent, and without the maturing experience of combat in war, he slides along as owner of a Cadillac agency (presumably his father's gift), getting by, as he always has, on charm and luck. It had gone well enough in the prosperous years of the late 1920's, but it is 1930 and things are changing. He had needed $10,000 but had exploited his charm and once-superior class position to borrow $20,000 from Harry Reilly, indebting himself to precisely the wrong man.

Now Julian needs more. He will always need more. Despite his sexual self-confidence, he conceives a completely irrational fear of Reilly as a rival for Caroline's affections because, in

Julian's fevered imagination, Reilly's money has invested him with a potency which his own looks, background, and manners cannot match. His ineptitude with money becomes increasingly one of his major fears and an irritant to his latent anger, and money in O'Hara's fictional world is power. Upon money depends respectability and social acceptance; its possession and wise use also testify to the virtue of its possessor. To Julian insolvency becomes more than a mistake, it seems a sin—one more added to the overwhelming burden of guilt and self-disgust he already bears. We see, then, that his suicide springs from no sudden compulsion, no quirk, no command of the gods. His fate flows, as it does in the creations of most serious novelists, from the wellsprings of his character.

With all these faults, what makes Julian important? Why is his end tragic, or at the very least poignant? We note something of its significance in the way Caroline thinks of him after his death: as a young officer who had died in the war, with his own inimitable gallantry of attitude, manner, and gesture (293-94). Moreover, he is considered a true gentleman by the two men in Gibbsville least likely to romanticize about people, Al Grecco and Ed Charney, who trade in other men's vices, as well as by such other tough, experienced men as Harry Reilly, Father Creedon, and Lute Fliegler.

In other words, there is an indefinable winningness about Julian, a finer substance underneath the glitter. One might almost say that he has an aura of beauty about him, or of the potentially beautiful: a zest, a joy in living, a sense of the comic, a spontaneity. He reminds us in part of Fitzgerald's people, of Dick Diver in *Tender Is the Night;* like him, he has the gift of stimulating others by his very presence, of bringing them an illusion of happiness. Like him, too, his grace is curiously emphasized by his very flaws. For Gibbsville, Julian represents the glamor, the *noblesse oblige,* the easy carelessness of the high aristocratic life; and his spark glows all the more brightly against the grey Gibbsville backdrop overcast by the lengthening shadows of Depression. His tragedy, and by implication man's, is that he lacks the self-knowledge, the nobility of character, the moral stamina to sustain the surface beauty.

Just as the themes and events of *Appointment in Samarra* operate on several different levels, so does O'Hara's narrative method work toward the effect of simultaneity and felt life. We find in O'Hara's first novel one of his fundamental techniques: that of the concurrent use of varying points of view, or what will hereafter be called the *shifting perspective*. An analysis of the book's opening chapter will seek to describe this technique and to demonstrate how it interacts with other elements of the work.

The novel's first three words are: "Our story begins...." That is, the reader hears a narrator's voice and is guided by an impartial observer's cues. It is the familiar, traditional mode of the editorial omniscient.[6] However, O'Hara quickly removes his own obvious presence and melts into the selective omniscient; first briefly entering the mind of Lute Fliegler and then that of his wife Irma. Irma's thoughts become the narrative projection for the remainder of the scene. This technique resembles stream-of-consciousness but differs from it in that the reader does not directly confront the inchoate outpouring of Irma's thoughts and emotions, as he does with Joyce's Molly Bloom; instead, he hears them as they are first filtered through the mind of a nearly invisible neutral observer. Through Irma the reader gets the middle-class attitude of the not-yet-rich but socially ambitious family, replete with its prejudices and snobberies. Further, through Irma one is convinced of the quality of her husband, Lute, as a strong, loyal, sensible, stable man. Since Julian later measures himself against men like Lute, one must know what he represents. Finally, the spontaneous and affectionate sexuality which the Flieglers enjoy symptomizes the security and harmony of their marriage, conjugal *love* as well as desire—yet another contrast to the Englishes. Scene I of Chapter One closes with Irma thinking about the country club dance and wondering whether Julian and Caroline English are fighting again.

Scene II shifts to the dance, rendered by means of a dual point of view: an unobtrusively editorial-omniscient depiction of the people at the dance and the introduction of Harry Reilly telling an off-color joke downstairs in the smoking room, followed by the shift into the mind of Julian English at the very instant it entertains the notion of throwing a drink into Reilly's face. O'Hara then momentarily returns to the dance upstairs, creating a brief but telling interval of suspense, before the reader learns that Julian has indeed surrendered to his absurd impulse.

Scene III shifts to Al Grecco, the young hoodlum who works for the local bootlegger and crime-boss, Ed Charney. From the mental processes of Grecco, the reader is apprised that Julian enjoys the liking and the respect of the Charney-Grecco element in Gibbsville. He is further apprised of the town's power-structure, and that every "respectable" man can be either bought or silenced if he dares oppose Charney. Through Al Grecco's eyes, the aftermath of Julian's disastrous act at the club is first presented. Grecco has always respected Julian for his expert handling of an automobile; now, on his way home, Julian wheels his car recklessly and abusively (a foreshadowing of his more general loss of control, already under way), while his wife sits furiously silent beside him. As Al drives down Latenengo Street, his greeting to the darkened houses of the prosperous fully represents his worm's-eye vantage point and serves as a fittingly ironic ending for the chapter: "Merry Christmas, you stuck-up bastards!"

Thus in Chapter One O'Hara has offered a representation of the novel's milieu, a synopsis of its situation, a foreshadowing of its outcome, and an insight into some of its characters and con-flicts. The reader also knows through O'Hara's astonishing dexterity in his handling of point-of-view that he is in the hands of a craftsman. Certainly the placing of the crisis of the novel at its very start is a bold and effective gambit. The remainder of the novel continues to build one's admiration for O'Hara's skill; for, with the use of varying scenes and the shifting perspec-tive, O'Hara employs yet other techniques.

For example, in Chapter Five O'Hara slows the action to insert a flashback summarizing the life, especially the romantic life, of Caroline, Julian's wife. Not only does this chapter serve the immediate purpose of exposition, of illuminating certain aspects of Caroline's character and of her marriage, but in the structure of the entire novel it also serves a vital esthetic function. In the first four chapters O'Hara has set down a series of swift-running episodes which build to an almost excruciating sense of gathering doom. Such rapid movement and cumulative tension could not be maintained, nor should they be, if the novel is to hold its reader to the end. Therefore, in the more leisurely told chapter recounting Caroline's past, a chapter shrewdly placed at exactly the halfway mark in the novel, O'Hara achieves stasis by changing the mood and pace and by pulling the reader away from the "now" of the action.

The same effect, the alternation of action and inaction, of dramatic scene with narration and description, of violence and stasis, is also maintained throughout the novel by O'Hara's strategic insertion of little anecdotes about the characters or items of local history. At times, in fact, *Appointment in Samarra* has something of the construction of the pattern or tapestry novel in which characters and events are at first presented individually, seemingly without the least relationship to one another, only later to be woven together into a whole, large, variegated fabric.

Finally, to O'Hara's accomplishment of a multi-layered rendition of reality, must be added his success in individual scenes, notably those in which he produces a completely convincing sense of lived experience: the sensation of hangover which seems to saturate the entire novel; the absurd wisdom of drunkenness; the almost Surrealistic scene of the events at the Stage Coach Inn; the tactile response to putting a gun in one's mouth; the flow of thoughts in the mind of a bereaved woman; and, most unforgettable of all, the montage of fear and self-disgust in Julian's whiskey-stimulated imagination just before his suicide, as he visualizes himself going down, down. One notes the adroitness with which O'Hara moves from external observation to interior monologue, altering the reader's stance from that of observer to participant. We begin by listening to O'Hara approximate Julian's thoughts about himself, but before we finish the passage we have witnessed Julian's conjuration of all the damning, humiliating whispers and rebuffs he fancies as his future:

He didn't want to go back and make a more definite break with Caroline. He didn't want to go back to anything, and he went from that to wondering what he wanted to go to. Thirty years old. "She's only twenty, and he's thirty. She's only twenty-two, and he's thirty. She's only eighteen, and he's thirty and been married once, you know. You wouldn't call him young. He's at least thirty. No, let's not have him. He's one of the older guys. Wish Julian English would act his age. He's always cutting in. His own crowd won't have him. I should think he'd resign from the club. Listen, if you don't tell him you want him to stop dancing with you, then I will. No thanks, Julian, I'd rather walk. No thanks, Mr. English, I haven't much farther to go. Listen, English, I want you to get this straight. Julian, I've been a friend of your family's for a good many years. Julian, I wish you wouldn't call me so much. My father gets furious. You better leave me out at the corner, becuss if my old man. Listen, you leave my sister alone. Oh, hello, sweetie, you want to wait for Ann she's busy now be down in a little while. No liquor, no meat, no coffee, drink plenty of water, stay off your feet as much as possible, and we'll have you in good shape in a year's time, maybe less" (276-77).

It is one of the better passages of its kind in American fiction. The novel which contains it, *Appointment in Samarra,* was indeed an auspicious beginning for John O'Hara.

II A Rage to Live:

The Rich, Compulsion, and Social History

After *Appointment in Samarra* and except for occasional short stories, O'Hara turned to other locales and life-styles for his material; he did not return to Pennsylvania in his fiction until fifteen years later. With the publication of *A Rage to Live* in 1949, O'Hara was home again. Moreover, with that novel O'Hara launched, in effect, a new career, which even now continues on the same course. The most spectacular phase of the new career is its astonishing productivity: fifteen volumes in as many years. Another phase is the heavy emphasis, much to the good, upon Pennsylvania characters and setting. A third phase, with mixed results, is the penchant for social history.

Beginning with *A Rage to Live*, O'Hara has been preoccupied with a sense of the past, with the attempt to capture not only individual lives and the places and events involved in them but also to encompass a whole milieu. In *A Rage to Live* he peels away the social layers of a medium-size American city, Fort Penn (Harrisburg), and looks into the human mechanisms which control it and which lend it significance. "I couldn't have written it at the time I did *Appointment in Samarra,*" O'Hara later told an interviewer. "The earlier books were special books about specialized people; but this is the big one, the over-all one."[7]

The core of the novel is—as it always must be—a special tale about specialized people, in this case the tale of Grace Caldwell Tate whose inability to control her sexual passions on a few crucial occasions results in the tragic destruction of her marriage and in the loss of what is best in her life. Surrounding this core, and for the most part tightly integrated with it, is the chronicle of Fort Penn and the Caldwell family, the city's leading family in its influence on the tone and style of the upper class, from approximately 1900 to 1920, with most of the novel's action concentrated between 1917 and 1920.

Perhaps the most remarkable aspect of this large created world, twenty years in the life of an American city, is O'Hara's depiction of the money, power, and privilege of the highest aristocracy. In contrast to the merely well-to-do characters portrayed in *Appointment in Samarra*, the millionaires of *A Rage to Live* are virtually above punishment from the social consequences of their actions. Plainly and simply, they can have almost anyone or anything they want. As is the case with Grace, when there are consequences, they will be personal rather than social.

This is not to say that the rich constantly exercise their prerogatives; in fact, they remain prerogatives only so long as they are not unduly exploited. But in electing a man to office, effecting or forestalling a civic project, saving a man's life or taking it (not by murder but by the kind of economic, political, and social pressures which make his existence intolerable), setting or ending a fashion—all these fall within the power of the rich, the strong, the established, and the well-connected.

Two brief examples, or episodes, illustrate the means of communication and the mailed-fist-within-the-kid-glove methods of the power élite. In 1902 one Louis Baum, a clerk, kills his wife and her lover, an Italian physician, when he catches them *in flagrante delicto*. Because Baum is a nobody and because the man he has killed has considerable prominence among the city's Italian population, Baum faces a death sentence, or at the least life imprisonment. At this point, certain events occur behind the scenes. In brief, a lady of solid family but scant means who happens to be Baum's cousin, genteelly blackmails Emily Caldwell (Grace's mother) into persuading her husband Will to intercede in Baum's behalf. Will Caldwell then asks Desmond O'Connell, the town's most influential lawyer to do so; and, because no one refuses a Caldwell, O'Connell takes Baum's case and gets him off with a reduced charge and sentence.

Another episode occurs late in the novel. Roger Bannon, the Irish building contractor once Grace's lover, speaks rudely to her on the telephone. Outraged, Brock Caldwell (Grace's brother) takes it upon himself to put Bannon in his place by arranging a series of "little conferences" for him. First, Bannon's bank threatens to call in his note. Next, Bannon finds that the city health department wishes to "discuss" the construction of sewers in a subdivision Bannon has built. Then word begins to circulate about the widely known but never publicly exposed episode of Bannon's assault upon a prostitute. This increasing pressure, added to a public snub by Grace in one of the town's most fashionable places, sends the tormented, frustrated Bannon off in a blind and soon-drunken rage that causes an auto wreck in which he kills himself and his latest mistress. As Bannon's epitaph, Brock says to Grace: "I know how to deal with scum like that. Like one of your horses. You have to be boss from the beginning, the very first time he acts up."[8]

These episodes reinforce a remark made late in the novel by a state trooper who has been sent to guard Grace against another attack by the hysterical wife of one of Grace's lovers. Discovering the officer there in the dark, Grace considerately sets out a midnight snack for him, telling him: "I'll put some coffee in a thermos and some sandwiches on the kitchen table." Later he enters to find an entire coffee service and a large platter containing a dozen neatly wrapped sandwiches. With the mixture of awe, resentment, and admiration typical of the lower-class attitude toward the rich, the trooper says: "Christ, a full meal. These bastards know how to live" (584). That remark is, in fact, an ironically ambiguous statement of the novel's major theme.

What happens to Baum, saved by the rich, and Bannon, destroyed by them, conveys only one aspect of it. Wealth, power, and status also impose their own burdens. As Grace's son says shortly after his father's death: "It *in*tails [*sic*] responsibility. Daddy told me that. If you have more advantage it *in*tails more responsibility" (343). Part of the responsibility of the rich is to carry their heads high, regardless of circumstances; to bury their dead without hysteria; always to conduct themselves in public with modest but unshakable dignity (as Grace must make her public appearances with composed mien no matter what tragedy or scandal surrounds her); to insure that the politicians steal only small sums and do not throttle the town's spirit and well-being; to recognize and reward able people from the lower classes and to help the right ones climb; to protect the good name of their own class and always to stand together in solidarity.

Another facet or extension of the state trooper's remark about the rich—perhaps its most obvious facet—concerns the opportunity for gracious living which money affords. Money and unchallenge-able social position permit Brock Caldwell and Sidney Tate to spend their time as they wish: Brock in discreet dissipation and dabbling in local history; Sidney in running the Caldwell farm. In neither case does a family's economic existence depend upon the labor of these men. Their fortunes grow largely by them-selves. The Caldwells and the Tates have both freedom and the taste, and the means to savor it to the fullest. However, they take their pleasures with restraint, even Grace—although with occasional lapses. Because they are what they are, some of the ease, orderliness, and style of their lives adheres to the com-munity and adorns it. The event with which the novel opens, the Fourth of July Festival held on the Tate Farm, borrows much of its warmth, color, and gaiety directly from the fact that it is being held on the Tate Farm; and the thousands who attend the Festival bask in the glow of the Caldwell-Tate hospitality. For a while, the obscure and humble are also permitted to know how to live.

Further, as Fitzgerald observed, money makes its possessors strong where others are weak and enables them to escape the consequences of their sins in ways that the poorer cannot. For, although O'Hara's rich suffer consequences, they suffer them privately (more of this in a moment). When one considers that Grace Tate becomes the subject of public scandal twice in three years, that all her friends know that she has been the sexual playmate of an Irish building contractor, and that absolutely nothing happens to Grace—not a snub, not a rebuke—the reader realizes just how potent inherited family money and high station can be. A man or woman of lesser position would be as much harassed and damaged by the community reaction (employer, business associates, social organizations) as by whatever ill effects accrued within his own conscience and his own house-hold. It must also be noted that, in his demonstration of the strength of the upper class, O'Hara superbly integrates his depic-tion of the rich of Fort Penn with the individual story of Grace Caldwell Tate; in the process, he achieves some of his most vibrant writing.

The situation offers further evidence that O'Hara is not the wholly deterministic portrayer of a social system which crushes all who dare to trespass its rules. In *A Rage to Live*, as in *Appointment in Samarra*, the sins of the rich and beautiful come *home* to rest. It is less what their peers or social protocols do to them than what happens between themselves and their loved ones which alters their lives. Only one person ever makes Grace regret her affair with Bannon, and that is her husband, who rejects her with disgust and disdain. Society remains an abstraction until it speaks through one person's voice, that of someone bound to the transgressor by the strongest human ties. And at this point the money and power of the rich cease to function to their benefit; for, in their private lives, the rich are no more proof against carnal temptations than the poor. Despite their public poise and dignity, O'Hara's rich remain human animals, subject to compulsion and instinct, as the behavior of Grace Caldwell Tate well illustrates. Thus, the novel's epigraph: "You purchase Pain with all that Joy can give,/And die of nothing but a Rage to live."[9]

Sexual desire is the strongest of these passions; in this way Grace is kin to Julian English. Or, since the hunger for money is something Grace never knows, sex remains. Although Grace is not a "nymphomaniac," as more than one reviewer called her, and is not even "promiscuous" by any strict definition of the word, she does at moments fall captive to her passions—overriding all ideals, rules, control. With the forthrightness which is one of her most commendable traits, she herself admits this enslavement: "There's very little admirable about me," she tells Dr. O'Brien, who has come to treat her youngest child stricken with polio. "I'm ashamed of myself. I couldn't help that affair, any more than Sidney could help getting sick, and Billy" (339). And later she rebuffs a man who tries to possess her: "I'm sorry . . . It has to be love with me, Paul. Or the other so much that I don't know where it comes from, and can't help it" (425). This fact of uncontrollable lust is one of the novel's major concerns and one of the facts of human behavior that it most tellingly illustrates.[10]

Yet another fact, inseparable from the first and demonstrated with equal or greater impact, is that of the consequences of lust. Or, to make the novel's statement into a kind of syllogism, *A Rage to Live* demonstrates that in the most basic matters people often cannot help what they do, although life is such that they are judged for what they do and punished for it—with the final irony that they are not changed for the better nor instructed by the punishment. Those are the bitter terms by which humans must live.

If the power of compulsion is embodied by Grace, then the need for control finds expression in Sidney Tate, the chief spokesman for the standards by which men's lives *ought* to be conducted. Sidney, a rare man, is kind, just, sane, intelligent, although not without imperfection. Furthermore, he represents the aristocrat at his best, for his wealth and education have sensitized him without making him effete. When he and Grace finally talk about her affair with Bannon, he tells her that he, too, has known desire for other women and has had opportunities to indulge it, but that, unlike her, he has not:

> "But the difference is, you see in this world you learn a set of rules, or you *don't* learn them. But assuming you learn them, you stick by them. They may be no damn good, but you're who you are and what you are because they're your rules and you stick by them. And of course when it's easy to stick by them, that's no test. It's when it's hard to obey the rules, that's when they mean something. That's what I believe, and I always thought you did too. I'm the first, God knows, to grant that you, with your beauty, you had opportunities or invitations. But you obeyed the rules, the same rules I obeyed. But then you said the hell with them. What it amounts to is you said the hell with my rules, and the hell with me" (245).

Sidney's indictment of Grace contains a vitally important and fundamental ethical concept implicit in O'Hara's work; indeed, it may be the key to his entire ethical system. For example, James D. MacHardie in *From the Terrace* says to Alfred Eaton: "Marriage is first of all an exchange of vows. A contract. . . . To me the sanctity of marriage means the sanctity of the vows, the promises, the contract, the given word."[11] It should be obvious to anyone who reads O'Hara carefully, although astonishingly it has not been obvious to many of his critics, that O'Hara presents eloquent spokesmen for traditional morality. His characters sin, but they also pay heavily—not in an afterlife but here and now—to themselves and the people they love. And, as Sidney's words to Grace imply, payment is exacted not because the transgressor has broken some abstract commandment, but because he has in his transgression violated some basic human relationship, some vow, some commitment on which all other phases of the relationship depend.

It is, therefore, a wholly humanistic morality which O'Hara creates (although one is tempted to speculate that it takes its impulse in part from the Catholicism which O'Hara professed as a boy and later rejected) and which he affirms. In this sense O'Hara is strict, even puritanical. But he is also pragmatic. His moral codes have meaning only if and as people live them; they must be exercised to be true. As Sidney's speech further implies, men's rules are not external to them. They become part of people and lend them vitality and identity, if men engender the rules by practicing them. Any transgression of those rules wreaks a dual destruction: it destroys the basis of faith and confidence upon which all personal relationships must be founded, especially those between husband and wife, parent and child, friend and friend; and it demolishes the very *personality* of the relationship; it is a rejection of the other.

At moments in O'Hara's fiction characters attempt to read a larger, a cosmic meaning into their acts and the consequences of them; that is, to lift those acts to a religious dimension. But, true to his wholly secular vision, O'Hara permits his characters no such comfort. As Grace says to Dr. O'Brien, just after her youngest child falls gravely ill: "Maybe I'm not *being* punished. Maybe I didn't do anything to deserve punishment. Why punishment, anyway? Payment, maybe, but not punishment. The law of averages, as much pleasure as you get pain. You're trying to make me think like a Catholic, and I don't even believe in God" (340). Thus Grace must bear her afflictions, or consequences, or punishments, or results of the law of averages, without any support other than what she draws from her own strength of morale.

Grace's sins are all the more striking because of her quality. Like Julian English, her destiny is significant because she is exceptional. Like him, she is beautiful and damned. What Grace Caldwell represents can be inferred from what others think of her. Even as he condemns her, Sidney says of her: "I've always admired you as well as loved you. You always had courage and independence. Real guts. Not only physical. You have as much of that as any man. But courage of the spirit" (252). Later, Hollister falls in love with her as much for her personal characteristics and virtues as for her physical beauty. Mary Kemper, a minor but not insignificant character in the novel, more than admires Grace; she reveres her: "In Mary's eyes the best was not enough for Grace; it had to be the right best. Grace was the best-

CARNEGIE LIBRARY
LIVINGSTONE COLLEGE
SALISBURY, N. C. 28144

dressed woman in Fort Penn—but *without trying*. She was the handsomest—*but without caring*. She was the kindest—*but expected nothing*. She did everything the right way—*but without stopping to think about it*" (518). In short, Grace (the name is not accidental) embodies most of what a woman can aspire to be, except in one salient quality: her sexual passion is that of a female, not a lady.

Grace's one great flaw may be singularly unbecoming, but she is not the only flawed character. None of O'Hara's major characters escape blemish. Even the novel's most admirable character, Sidney, devoted husband and father, with all his virtues and attractiveness, has his shortcomings. Perhaps his greatest or at least his most tragic is his lack of compassion—the inability to forgive Grace for her error. To forgive her would have been the consummate test of his love and his code. Unfortunately, his code does not reach quite all the way to forgiveness, although she humbly asks it of him.

Grace had failed him first and most seriously, just as Julian had first failed Caroline in *Appointment in Samarra;* but the failure is compounded and made permanent by the lack of understanding and compassion in the betrayed. Even as the sinner cannot hold his impulses in check, so those he has wronged cannot restrain their outrage and contempt. In Sidney's case the sin is that of pride nourished by his own self-sufficiency and solitariness. As Grace says of him to a friend, just before her dreadful secret is brought into the open, "I've done what he would never do. He believes all those things you're brought up to believe. Honor. Vows. Promises. The Golden Rule" (237). True to her analysis, Sidney cannot understand her actions; his earlier idealism, now violated, has soured into disillusionment, disenchantment, bitterness.

With all its seriousness, its memorable dramatic scenes, its frequent profundity, the shrewdness of its perception of behavior, *A Rage to Live* nevertheless fails to equal *Appointment in Samarra* in its total achievement. Superficially one might say, as the critics frequently do of O'Hara's books, that it is too long. Granted, *A Rage to Live* struggles under the weight of thickly detailed descriptions of artifacts, cars, clothes, furniture, houses, and is interrupted by long family genealogies and historical reminiscences. But this flaw is not the major one because the writing in such excursions is taut, sprightly, varied, and lucid;

even when they intrude into the narrative, O'Hara always has the skill to bring us back to the main line of his story.

No, O'Hara's obsession with things and with history is not his main fault here; that obsession, however, does signal what is essentially wrong with *A Rage to Live*. The basic flaw is structure. To be specific, *A Rage to Live* really ends after Book Three, with the death of Grace's husband and youngest son. Her marriage is the most important thing in her life, as marriage and love are generally the most vital elements in the lives of O'Hara's people; and the deaths of her marriage and of two of her loved ones are the most important events that happen to her. Furthermore, these deaths complete the novel's major action. All else must be anticlimactic.

As Henry James and others have demonstrated, anticlimax can be an effective literary device, but O'Hara spreads the anticlimax over two entire sections in his novel. He might in this instance have profitably studied his master Fitzgerald in *Tender Is the Night,* who in a few chilling pages briefly sketches Dick Diver's final dissolution, leaving the detail to the reader's imagination. But, propelled by the historian's impulse rather than by the novelist's, O'Hara goes on and on, writing an additional two hundred and forty pages whose chief interest is no longer Grace Caldwell Tate but Fort Penn. In these pages *A Rage to Live* ceases to be a specialized tale about specialized people and becomes, instead, the fictive chronicle of a city.

The reason for this misfortune is probably O'Hara's attempt as a Realist to make his books like life itself, for life continues long after its most important experiences are past. Yet just at this point the Realist must give way to the artist. Art may be an imitation of life but it can hardly be an exact replication of it. Even if the Realist believes, as O'Hara does, that life itself is pointless and unstructured, all the more reason his art must be pointed and structured. Furthermore, O'Hara the historian cannot function effectively apart from O'Hara the novelist. Earlier it was suggested that milieu, character, and action in much of *A Rage to Live* were inseparable, and, with this unity in mind, we can come to a judgment of the novel.

Approximately two thirds of *A Rage to Live*'s nearly six hundred pages comprise a strong novel in which milieu, character, and action form an esthetic whole depicting vital human relationships surging under the surface of a convincing material reality. In these pages O'Hara works at the top of his form, which is to say that he approaches greatness. As for the rest, regardless of its frequent merit and interest, it is, from the standpoint of a complete artistic achievement, a lamentable waste.

III Ten North Frederick:
Failure and the Well-Adjusted Man

In *Appointment in Samarra* and *A Rage to Live* it is plain that O'Hara has a predilection for characters and situations which dramatize the anguish of those who achieve beneath their own ideals and possibilities. F. Scott Fitzgerald, a writer who seems to compel frequent comparison with John O'Hara, also once said that he was obsessed by the theme of failure and that all his stories had this twist. What is true for Fitzgerald and O'Hara has been true as well for much distinguished American fiction of the mid-twentieth century. Asked why, in a country so rich and powerful, a country whose popular creed depends upon Success and Happiness, American writers are so persistently concerned with failure, misery, and loss, James T. Farrell replied: "A happy man has no history."[12] Indeed, the Realist looks first to the unhappy man for his material. As the Realist sees life, unhappiness and failure comprise the larger portion of man's destiny—are the most urgent facts of his condition.

In order to more clearly depict failure and more sharply define it, the Realist has usually chosen as his subject the average man, the commonplace: the wife of a small-town doctor, a businessman, a shopkeeper, a student. Or, if he inclines toward Naturalism, the writer selects such characters as the vagrant, the drug addict, the dispossessed farmer. Only rarely does the Realist or Naturalist single out as the basis for his exploration into failure an intelligent and attractive man of respected family, a successful attorney, a devoted husband and father, and a millionaire counted among the leading citizens of a small American city. Yet O'Hara portrays just such a man in *Ten North Frederick,* Joseph Chapin, of the place the writer knows best, Gibbsville, Pennsylvania; and he makes his story an extended ironic commentary on Success and Happiness.

As the novel unfolds, Joseph Chapin's advantages are dispelled one by one: his personal attractiveness becomes of no consequence to him; his intelligence falls short of perceiving that his wife wishes more to possess than to love him and that other men manipulate him to their profit; his family name remains honorable only because its ugly secrets are screened from public view; his prestigious legal practice contributes nothing of significance either to the community, to individuals in trouble, or to the law itself; his devotion to wife and children is painfully misapplied and ill-requited; his wealth serves only his own and his family's personal needs; his leadership as a citizen is attested to by the number of important people at his funeral, although they are men whose lives he has generally little affected.

One might infer from this summary that Joe Chapin is a character not worth writing about because he has been too obtuse to confront his failures. However, among the strengths of *Ten North Frederick* is its demonstration that, tragically, Joe Chapin does come to know, late in his life: precisely when he might look back over what he has achieved and in old age bask in the memory of earlier triumphs, he must face the cold desolation of failure recognized and acknowledged. His wife of more than thirty years hates him and assists in his suicide; his son has become a bitter, hard-drinking ne'er-do-well; his beautiful and loving daughter's life has been disfigured by an annulled marriage and an abortion, both of which he willed; his political ambitions to be lieutenant-governor of Pennsylvania and ultimately President of the United States have turned grotesque; and the one instance of true and passionate love he experiences comes to him as an old man, with a girl of his daughter's age, in a situation impossible of fruition. And so Joe Chapin drinks himself to death in the quiet, gentlemanly, and gradual way in which he has lived his life. There is no tragic hero's sudden, violent, splendid end for him. Rather, he undergoes a deterioration and disintegration, portrayed by O'Hara with terrifying accuracy.

This reprise of Chapin's failures may seem to imply that O'Hara condemns Joe Chapin and men like him for what they are, or perhaps are not. But, if the reader can surmise a judgment behind O'Hara's impersonal narrative method, he judges with compassion and understanding, as the novel's closing indicates: "And one man's life is more than any one person can fully remember, just one man's life, and so we remember what we can, what we are reminded of, what gives us pleasure or sadness to remember."[13]

From one vantage place, Joseph Chapin seems a victim of forces, a man whose destiny has been determined by his rearing, by his social role, and by his physical and emotional needs. From this position, O'Hara appears to be a Naturalist. But Joe also exercises free will; in the four most important decisions of his life, he has and uses the power to choose. They are: his selection of wife, his decision to strive for high office, his handling of his daughter's marriage and pregnancy, and his romance with Kate Drummond. To compare Joe to some earlier O'Hara protagonists, Julian English and Grace Tate, is immediately to see the difference and to conclude also that in *Ten North Frederick* O'Hara is more the Realist than the Naturalist. Julian, too, can exercise will, but chance and impulse nevertheless affect him at critical moments in his life; and Grace falls completely under the sway of her own compulsions just often enough to ruin her. In sharp contrast, Joe's major resolutions all depend on other than purely physical and emotional needs; indeed, his tragedy may be traced directly to the functioning (and malfunctioning) of his intelligence.

In his choice of his wife Edith, Joe takes a woman suitable to his social station and professional ambitions, as well as one who gratifies his concept of self. Not beautiful and hardly good (although she deludes him to the contrary), she is shrewd, subtle, tough, and poised; and she fulfills her role completely to his satisfaction for more than thirty years. If Joe is not sensitive enough to realize until too late how clever and selfish she is, he at least has sufficient strength to frustrate her chief design: to possess him completely. Only when she realizes that he has evaded her grasp does she come to hate him, and by then his life nears its close. Thus in his marriage, Joe determines the course of events as much as he is determined by them.

In his decision to embark upon a political career, and more important in his manner of doing so, he makes only one serious mistake: he errs in thinking he can do it on his own by creating a personal following based on his prestige and popularity. The way his world works, Joe could have succeeded only by first subordinating himself to the local boss, Mike Slattery, and then by functioning under Mike's strategy and within the party machine.

When Joe attempts to cope with his daughter's hasty marriage and arranges an abortion, he reacts with a mistaken notion of social propriety, of status; he concludes that, because her husband is a mere musician and of humble Italian origin, Ann is fated to a low, miserable life. Once more he does not realize until too late that marital happiness may depend upon elements other than wealth and family background. But whatever Joe might be accused of in this instance—snobbery, intolerance, patriarchal tyranny—he cannot be accused of viciousness. He acts not only from the sense of the decencies and proprieties as he has conceived and practiced them, but also from an honest albeit misguided idea of a parent's duty toward his child. The annulment and abortion are primarily for Ann's sake, so he believes.

Finally, in his love for Kate Drummond he displays his strongest will. From the outset he knows this relationship can only be a transient one, and he conducts himself accordingly. True, Kate has something to do with the course of the affair, but by herself she would not have been strong enough to resolve it. In fact, were it not for Kate's specific invitation, Joe would have left her with simply the verbal expression of his love, without physical consummation. She would have become his mistress if he so wished it; he would have refused because of the hardship such an arrangement would impose upon *her*. Even in the one great passion of his life, his principles and life-style prevail over whatever he might feel or desire.

The difference between Joe and other men, those with less will and self-respect, is summarized in a conversation with a minor character, one Paul Donaldson. Donaldson, who habitually philanders, justifies his actions on the basis of his physical needs. Joe argues that moral commitments and respect for one's mate have precedence over bodily demands. The conversation concludes:

> "If I had to do it over again there isn't a single piece of tail I'd want to give up. So I guess I consider myself a happy man. God knows I don't consider *you* a happy man. You go ahead and consider me a f - - - - - - hypocrite, but I consider you a miserable, unhappy bastard. You never got anything out of life, and, boy, you wouldn't know how to start now."
>
> "But that's assuming I'd *want* to start now," said Joe (365).

Therefore, the sum of the life of Joe Chapin partakes both of what he could and did control, and of what was beyond his power and knowledge. Accordingly, as a predominantly Realistic rather than Naturalistic work *Ten North Frederick* offers a less graphic demonstration of the operation of sex and money upon character than in most other O'Hara novels. Money is a relatively small factor here. Because Joe has money and has always had it, its possession influences him little; unlike the rich of *A Rage to Live*, Joe's fundamental conservatism permits no use of money as instrument or toy. Although one of his ambitions, to leave his wife and two children each a million dollars upon his death, is frustrated by the crash of 1929, the loss of nearly two million dollars neither ruins Joe (he has a million left) nor cripples him emotionally. Likewise, O'Hara avoids close scrutiny of anyone else in the novel whose biography is greatly affected by money. The fact that Joe Chapin has money constitutes part of his prestige in Gibbsville but not the whole of it; nor can all Joe's money buy what he most desires: high political office and his children's happiness. His political aspirations cost him one hundred thousand dollars, for which he gets nothing in return except some belated insight into the true nature of politics and the manner of his own victimization.

Similarly, sex, however present elsewhere in O'Hara's fiction, plays a minor role in the life of Joe Chapin. Although Edith Chapin has a selfish and eager sexuality (including an element of perversion) which demands release, she receives gratification in the conjugal bed, except for one solitary episode in her long married life. Joe, too, finds his mate more than adequate to his bodily needs, which are not extraordinary. Other characters may have more than their share of passion (Ann Chapin), or some peculiarity of behavior (Lloyd Williams), but nowhere in *Ten North Frederick* does O'Hara show that one's lusts dominate one's life, as they did Julian English's or Grace Tate's. O'Hara neither reverses his attitude about the force of sex in the shaping of character and destiny, nor portrays it less candidly. He merely emphasizes it less and treats it proportionately as but one of several factors working upon his people. Once more, O'Hara the Realist prevails in *Ten North Frederick* over O'Hara the Naturalist.

Another of the shaping factors, reminiscent of O'Hara's treatment in *Appointment in Samarra,* is the parent-child relationship.

Joe's faults as an adult can be traced at least in part to an imbalance in his rearing: too much indulgent love from the mother, not enough love and control from the father. This imbalance produces a coldness and remoteness in Joe, an egotism and arrogance so early instilled and so artfully formed that it was never a conscious or deliberate effect. From his father he might have learned what it meant to be humble, to fail, to be sensual; but the father abrogates his responsibilities toward the child by allowing his wife to dominate. Only on one occasion does the father share a real intimacy with the boy: just after he has taught Joe to swim by first throwing him into deep water and then entering the water with the terrified child and giving him instruction. Although Joe himself is a more attentive and affectionate father to his children, something goes wrong there also. Again a cold and ruthless mother is permitted to exert too much influence. Further, the child whom Joe loves best, his first-born Ann, he fails the most by not supporting her impetuous marriage and allowing it to work itself out. Instead, he destroys it. As for his son, Joe never reaches him at all. The boy's one talent and interest, to be a jazz pianist, is considered beneath notice or encouragement. Once more O'Hara has diagnosed his characters' ailments as stemming from a failure of love.

The strongest environmental force affecting Joe Chapin thus derives not from any single factor but from several: not sex alone nor money nor social position nor breeding, but the total of these. One feels, somehow, that the air breathed at Number Ten North Frederick Street in Gibbsville, Pennsylvania, and in the Chapin-McHenry law office, and indeed in whatever space Joseph Chapin inhabits, is stale, stuffy, deadening. His life, in the main, is proper, clean, disciplined, respectable, admirable to any outside observer, but it lacks urgency, vitality, intensity. Joe's vision of human conduct is lofty, yet there is an opacity to it.

O'Hara portrays this deadness succinctly and expertly by posing other, contrasting lives and by offering swift but telling glimpses into them: Carl and Amy Johnson, the school superintendent and his wife, climbing from the middle class into the town's élite; Conrad Yates, now mayor of Gibbsville but up from the farm and the Pennsylvania Dutch; Mike and Peg Slattery; even the Chapin's servants, Harry and Marian Jackson—all are capable of a vibrancy of feeling, of a depth of love, of a clarity of sight rarely if ever known to Joseph and Edith Chapin. As he often does, O'Hara has provided in this novel two people of lower-class, the Slatterys, whose relationship serves as a sort of standard of comparison for the Chapins. Not that the Slatterys are model human beings—far from it. They are too ruthlessly pragmatic, too limited to specific material goals to attract or to deserve emulation; but their marriage, their absolute devotion and loyalty to each other, their complete candor, their unblinking cognizance of the way things are, their total lack of pretense with or about each other—these are missing in the Chapin marriage. Whatever the Slatterys' defects as marriage partners or as individuals, they are at least fully *alive*. Even such a bounder as Lloyd Williams, who rises to a judgeship, refreshes the reader with his vitality, his bluntness, his rage to live.

O'Hara's purpose has thus been to single out the life of the sort of man one is tempted to admire, envy, imitate—a kind of Richard Cory who seems to the people on the pavement a finer and higher being—and to expose the flaws beneath the polished veneer. O'Hara shows the reader, as the Realist does at his best, the distance between human possibilities and actualities. Again and again he attempts to disabuse his audience of its illusions, assumptions, or shibboleths about such diverse matters as marriage, politics, characters, and personality—or about the relationship between the good and the evil, the weak and the strong. None of these hard-won observations provide much comfort to the optimist, idealist, or altruist. All are tough, thorny, disenchanted.

Ten North Frederick is an artistically accomplished book, as well as a sober and persuasive one. The twelfth volume to be published by O'Hara in a career then more than twenty years in progress, it was the first of his works to receive a major literary prize. Although as usual the reviewers were far from boisterous in their approval of the novel, a committee of eminent judges selected it for the National Book Award in fiction for 1955. The award citation read as follows: "A forthright, trenchant, and total picture of an American man, his family and his town. A masterpiece of construction, the work shows a remarkable control of material and a perfectly maintained distance from it. Tough-minded as usual, Mr. O'Hara has written a novel of emotional depth and moral conviction."[14]

The citation rightly stresses O'Hara's technical achievement; for, unlike *A Rage to Live,* this novel is both a large work and an economical one. Without the vividness of *Appointment in Samarra*, and containing no single scene or passage of great intensity and beauty, *Ten North Frederick* nevertheless works upon the reader through an unspectacular, cumulative, absorbing power. Among its virtues is structure. O'Hara uses no chapter divisions but creates the effect of flux by his employment of both narrative discourse and dramatic scene; furthermore, he gains a sense of variety and development by means of changing focus and shifting perspective. That is, he moves the reader from inside to outside, from character to character, and from place to place in what seems to be a smooth and continuous line but is actually a highly complex system which combines a frequent redeployment of the reader's attention with a variety of narrative modes.

For example, in the first sixty-three pages which cover some three hours in time, from just before Joe Chapin's funeral to the conversation of the family servants after the post-funeral reception at the Chapin home, one gets a superbly executed and wholly unobtrusive series of modulations in time, place, character, and point of view. O'Hara sets the opening scene in Edith Chapin's sitting room, where she receives the newspaper editor; then he moves to the funeral service at the church, where the reader enters the mind of Mike Slattery and overhears a conversation between Slattery's wife and daughter. Next, O'Hara focuses on the burial itself; then shifts to a limousine in the burial procession containing certain shrewd and influential men who discuss the dead man and his family; turns again to the Chapin home for an account of the post-funeral reception; then presents a series of dialogues between the surviving members of the Chapin family upstairs in their private quarters; travels next to the house of Carl and Amy Johnson for their comments on the proceedings; and finally returns to the kitchen at Ten North Frederick Street for further comment by the Chapins' servants. At this point the strands of the novel's narrative begin to reach too far to permit simple description.

What has been accomplished with this technique? First, O'Hara has foreshadowed in these pages virtually all the major actions and conflicts in the novel, excepting only Joe's late passion for Kate; the remainder of the book goes on to develop, detail, clarify, and cohere. Especially does it expand what was said in the limousine, that Edith and Joe Chapin and their marriage remain an enigma even to the sharpest observers. Second, O'Hara offers an insight into many of the chief characters, including the dead protagonist, and presents that insight by means of several narrative modes: his own direct statement; the central characters' thoughts, words, and deeds; and the reflections and reactions of other characters less deeply involved in the story. Third, O'Hara begins to study the ramifications and extensions of Joe Chapin's life, Chapin's importance not only in Gibbsville but his years at college, and the men (many of them distinguished) he has come to know in various connections.

As in *Appointment in Samarra*, O'Hara's shifting perspective—the backward and forward movement through space and time, and the variety and multiplexity of viewpoint—all resemble the technique of the pattern or tapestry novel; one in which the author brings some single character or aspect of his story to a certain phase of development, and continually repeats the process with other characters or phases, each time weaving a new thread into the frame until the threads begin to cross and form a pattern or tapestry. At last, the reader has the *whole* fabric before him and perceives how what appeared to be separate threads were actually components of a master design. The use of time also assists in this effect because O'Hara commences his story with the fictive present (1945), and so avails himself of the psychological immediacy of life as experienced in the Now; then, as is his habit, he returns to the past, structuring the remainder of the novel as a long flashback which relates what has transpired to create the present moment. Since the story spans the chronological distance from Joe Chapin's childhood, in the late years of the nineteenth century, to the day of his burial, it covers some fifty years and includes the Chapin family history for two generations.

With this combination of techniques O'Hara surrenders the element on which most merely popular writers depend: the conventional suspense of the "What happens next?" *Ten North Frederick* opens by declaring its hero is dead. Why read on? The answer is that O'Hara captivates the reader by suspense of a special sort: the suspense of the delayed revelation. We can know from the start the facts of what happened, but we can neither comprehend nor appreciate the truth of what happened until we have ascertained the *how* and *why* and *when*. Exactly the same technique is evidenced in the finely wrought opening chapter of *A Rage to Live:* when, at the end of the day of the festival with which the novel begins, Sidney Tate tells his wife, just as they are about to retire for the night, that he knows her awful secret, O'Hara leaves both Grace and the reader in dire anticipation of just what Sidney knows and what he will do about it.

Likewise, in *Ten North Frederick* for the first eighty-odd pages we are in the present, attending Joe's funeral and witnessing related scenes and dialogues. Then, O'Hara returns to the past and gradually moves forward in time until he has once again approached the present—to the moment when Joe and Edith terminate their marriage in all but the forms and when Joe will begin drinking himself to death. The last twenty pages illustrate how and why he has chosen this form of suicide; on the novel's penultimate page, the reader witnesses the physical death itself of internal hemorrhage induced by cirrhosis of the liver, and comes full circle to the day before the novel begins. And by that time we know not only what happened, but how and why and when; and we care.

IV   From the Terrace: *The Historical Fallacy*

From the Terrace, the story of Alfred Eaton who begins his life in a small Pennsylvania town, who suffers from the lack of his father's love, who attains eminence as a financier and government official, and who then finds himself in late middle age condemned to a trivial and hollow existence, is a massive novel of nearly nine hundred pages. It contains dozens of interesting and vividly drawn characters; its scope encompasses the first fifty years of the twentieth century, including both world wars; its narrative is often concerned with the two great themes of love and death; it sets forth many penetrating insights into the nature of individuals and of the social order; its hero moves in the upper reaches of two of the world's most interesting cities, New York and Washington. And yet, with all this, *From the Terrace* ultimately achieves less impact than all but O'Hara's weakest novels. Why?

The most cogent answer can probably be found in what I call "the historical fallacy." This fallacy is manifest in O'Hara's very intention, as set forth in the italicized foreword to the novel. In it O'Hara announces that he intends more than an account of one man's life, employs the significant word "chronicle," and enjoins the reader not to ponder the novel's purpose until it is finished but to concentrate instead on the lives and events contained in the narrative. In other words, O'Hara makes the startling request that the reader suspend his critical faculties, and an even more startling admission of the novelist's own daring in deliberately abnegating one of the prime essentials of fiction—selection. O'Hara tacitly promises that he will attempt to seize life itself, to create not a novel but a chronicle, not a story but a saga.

This commendably bold and grand attempt proceeds logically both from O'Hara's previous work and from the tradition of the Realistic-Naturalistic novel with its penchant for the *tranche de vie*. Unfortunately, the attempt in this case meets with failure; the slice of life has been cut too thick to be digestible. One can hardly call it a slice at all: a blob of life, a heap of life, a mass of life, perhaps. Even more emphatically than *A Rage to Live*, the first of O'Hara's sagas or chronicles, *From the Terrace* demonstrates the unhappy consequences of mistaken artistic ambitions.

O'Hara's failure to discipline his material is manifest in his narrative technique, for *From the Terrace* is simultaneously the most laborious of O'Hara's long fictions in the stupendous amount of research and sheer physical energy its writing must have entailed, and yet it is among the least sophisticated of his later books. Its methods evince little imagination. The point of view is, with few exceptions, the traditional editorial-omniscient. The time order is, also with few exceptions, the simple chronological one. There are only rare instances of such ordinarily effective O'Hara strategies as the delayed revelation. Nor do tone and movement vary greatly; everything is told in much the same manner and speed. Inevitably a kind of monotony, a dead level of sameness, prevails—an unfortunate effect further emphasized by the novel's exceeding length. As a result, the most intense scenes and shrewdest insights fail to stir the reader as they should. O'Hara refuses even to utilize such convenient devices as chapter and section divisions to mark off significant phases of his story. While this refusal is probably also part of his ambition to seize life as it is, the lack of signposts adds to the distraction of the faltering reader and further convinces him that the narrative itself allows no orderly division.

O'Hara himself often aggravates these defects in method by committing yet other errors. A particularly obvious example occurs at about the two-thirds point in the novel, in a passage set apart by an inch of white space and thus more sharply emphasized because of the rarity of such spacing in the book. The passage begins: "There followed a decade in Alfred's life that began with the birth of his daughter, ended with the death of a son, and was personated by a man for whom he had no respect or regard yet did not hate; but always in thinking about those ten years Alfred would see the pudgy, well-barbered face of Creighton Duffy." It then goes on to assert that, for the protagonist, Duffy became a personal symbol as meaningful as Hitler and Roosevelt were to others (565).

Because of its location and its portentous tone, and because the decade it mentions brings the reader close to the end of Eaton's history, the passage presumably stands as a thesis for the remainder of the tale. That is, the reader assumes from O'Hara's cue that Duffy, a minor character to this point, will now be enlarged and developed in his relationship to Alfred Eaton and in his function within the entire novel. Strictly speaking, this assumption is left unsatisfied; but the ensnared reader continues to search through the remaining three hundred pages for substantiation of the author's implied promise. Although Duffy moves closer to the center of the scene, he has only a minor place in the climactic events of the protagonist's life during those ten years: the maturing of Eaton's love for Natalie, the death of his son, the dissolution of his marriage, and his near-fatal illness. The passage cited above thus takes on, in retrospect, the hue of a very bright red herring. One wishes, in this case at least, that O'Hara had yielded in his customary refusal to permit editorial revision of his work and, like Thomas Wolfe, had accepted the services of a Maxwell Perkins to carve a novel from this mountain of prose.

There are other instances of unfulfilled intentions. Considering O'Hara's disposal of Tom Rothermel later in the novel, he gives the character disproportionate emphasis in the story's early portions. It appears that O'Hara had planned to juxtapose Tom Rothermel and Alfred Eaton, contrasting the poverty and struggle of the one with the financial ease and opportunity of the other, to illustrate the difference between the rich and the poor. Such a contrast could have been highly useful to O'Hara's ambition as social historian. As it turns out, the reader learns largely about the rich; for O'Hara soon ignores Rothermel except to revive him sporadically in order to remark his moral ruination. However, because O'Hara omits what happens to Tom that changes an honorable, hard-working youth into a gross and unscrupulous schemer, the reader is forced to accept on faith the repugnant person Tom mysteriously becomes.

Other characters enter and leave the narrative with no greater artistic justification, although such characters may be often mentioned and described at length. Templeton Avirett, the Washington lawyer; Henrietta McCandless, last of the five wives of Jack Tom Smith; and a lecherous California millionaire named Gratwin, whom we never meet, are but a few of the book's dispensable personages. In contrast, characters important to the novel sometimes get short shrift. For example, Ralph Benziger, Natalie's father, assumes in Alfred's mind from the first moment of their meeting something of divine status. Benziger is, the reader is told, one of the finest men Alfred ever knows: a model of moral and personal virtue. Yet one *sees* and *hears* Benziger for but a few pages; all other references to him are at secondhand.

However, the author's worst sins are committed in his treatment of the novel's major characters. To put it succinctly, after nine hundred pages which recount in detail fifty years of a man's life, the reader departs with a still dim and fragmented conception of Alfred Eaton and his motivations. Read superficially, the work seems to rest on the thesis "like father, like son." That is, *From the Terrace* seems to portray a man damaged by the neglect of his father to the extent that he becomes emotionally stunted, is unable to love deeply, and is compelled to give to his career the energy and passion rightfully belonging to human beings. A fierce, driving business competitor in his prime, he begins after his illness to deteriorate into an idler and an errand boy for his still-active friends; the reader leaves him in this pathetic condition at the novel's conclusion.

Unfortunately for both O'Hara and the reader, however, *From the Terrace* advances too much contrary evidence to allow the acceptance of either this configuration of Alfred's character or the nature of his fate. Whatever Eaton's faults, the most conclusive aspects of his history argue that he is a man capable of the deepest love, generosity, loyalty, and altruism—and that he is composed of too durable and fine a substance to be subject to any such deterioration. His deep involvement with his mother, even after he realizes she is an adulteress and an alcoholic, his abiding friendships with at least three men, his voluntary assumption of guilt for the deaths of two girls he has loved (although in both cases he is only circumstantially involved), his loyalty to his employer, his unwillingness to persecute his wife for her infidelities, his love for his children, his attempt to help a fallen aristocrat, his service to his country despite great sacrifice, and above all the intensity of his unswerving love for Natalie—all these factors testify that he is a man of conscience, feeling, and worth. How, then, can the reader believe that a man with such qualities, a man who has earned nearly three million dollars in high finance and performed with distinction as Assistant Secretary of the Navy, should so lose his moral stamina and capacity for self-appraisal that he would submit to the frivolous and humiliating existence O'Hara depicts as his lot?

To cite one last illustration of O'Hara's defective treatment of character, Mary St. John, who acts as the villainess of the story, is an even greater enigma. At first a properly reared young lady of beauty and integrity, she remains Alfred's loyal, loving wife until the birth of their first child. Then, without convincing motivation, she becomes an adulteress. One infidelity multiplies into many. Soon she employs gigolos to assuage her apparently inexhaustible sexual hunger and dabbles in homosexuality; finally, there remains almost no form of debauchery she has not tasted. Meanwhile, she has become verbal about her conduct and developed into a spokesman for a cult of sensation, like a character out of de Sade. And, while Mary pursues this orgiastic career, she somehow also manages to maintain a respectable, well-ordered home for her family and to play charming hostess to their aristocratic friends. Her debauches seemingly have no effect on her appearance, social position, or life-style (although her activities are hardly furtive); rather, they appear to heighten her allure and social poise. Without further discussion, we must pronounce such a creature plainly beyond belief as a character in any novel pretending to seriousness.

As Mary's situation indicates, *From the Terrace* also stresses its characters' sexual behavior to the limit of the reader's credibility. At best, it can be said for O'Hara that he continues to distinguish clearly between sex and love, deliberately employing a series of instances of base sensuality in order to heighten his characters' much more meaningful experiences of sexuality exalted by affection, love, and commitment. O'Hara summarizes the whole matter, and no doubt conveys his own views, in the dialogue between Alfred and Mary just before their divorce. Mary is an utter pragmatist. To her, sex is all; man lives by id alone. In contrast, Alfred, who affirms an ideal, replies that while man may often lose his control and behave as a beast, love is what gives value to his existence.

From the Terrace likewise illustrates on virtually every page O'Hara's continuing preoccupation with the rich. "I am fascinated by the rich and how they live, and I go with them every chance I get," he has written. "I guess I know as much about Society as any author today. . . . I am not in Society . . . but I have quite a few friends in Society, people I like a great deal because they are considerate, well-mannered, kind, undemanding, and have their own private hells."[15] *From the Terrace*, even more than *A Rage to Live*, bears witness to these statements. Most emphatically of all, O'Hara demonstrates very well in this novel that money assumes importance in inverse ratio to the quantity of it one owns. The less one has, the more one's life is affected by it—although, as Alfred Eaton's experience proves, money imposes its own special burdens: to name one, the prolongation of an unhappy marriage because divorce is both unseemly and expensive.

Finally, as I began by saying, *From the Terrace* climaxes O'Hara's ambition to be chronicler of his age. Of all his novels to date, this one has the widest sweep; it involves all the locales in which O'Hara himself has lived. Not only does the author track down the rich in their several habitats, but for the first time he ventures into a treatment of politics on the national scale. The New Deal and the Roosevelt administration during World War II receive much attention, while Roosevelt himself and other historical personages enter the story indirectly as minor characters. Furthermore, in a number of lengthy dialogues and descriptions O'Hara re-creates social history, striving to capture accurately certain moods and attitudes, just as he has faithfully transcribed for his readers the look and feel of things.

That O'Hara's self-conception as a historian has led him once more into egregious errors as an artist is everywhere patent, for the narrative repeatedly fails to dramatize and to vivify the mass of data with which it has been laden. In ironic contrast to the failure of O'Hara's grand historic design, he does best in *From the Terrace* what he usually does best: the Pennsylvania experience. The novel's early episodes set in Port Johnson—those involving the Eaton steel mill, Alfred's boyhood, and the various individuals and families pertinent thereto—are the work of an expert hand. O'Hara is never better than when he portrays the loneliness of a penurious boy at a country-club dance, or when he analyzes the effect of a strike upon the life of the community, or when he depicts what happens between husband and wife, parent and child. Precisely because the reader has this evidence of the author's craft before him, he mourns its demise in the subsequent, seemingly endless pages of the novel.

V Ourselves to Know: *Passions Spin the Plot*

It has been established that among O'Hara's basic structural devices is the delayed revelation: either the hinting of a crucial secret or the positing of some essential piece of information early in the narrative, followed by the gradual unfolding of the how and the why until at last the reader arrives at a complete disclosure. O'Hara's method might be described as circular, in contrast to the more frequent linear method which adheres to the familiar sequences of time and space, or to cause and effect. In any case, the key factor in the linear method is that the essential fact—the outcome, the climax—remains hidden until the end or near the end of the story so that it emerges from what has already been unfolded.

Although O'Hara's work exhibits many traditional aspects of the Realistic-Naturalistic tradition in both its concerns and its techniques, the circular method of *Ourselves to Know* lends it an experimental quality. Establishing early in the story a base of reference to serve later as its climax, the author moves away from it, seemingly at random, but then gradually returns to his starting point until the entire sweep of the narrative has been completed. Thus, even more directly than in *A Rage to Live* and in *Ten North Frederick*, O'Hara brings the delayed revelation into play in *Ourselves to Know*. On page six of this large novel we are informed that Robert Millhouser had killed his wife, was tried for it, and has long walked free; but not until the end does the reader learn exactly what did happen, or comprehend it.

Ourselves to Know also makes use of another of O'Hara's most effective techniques: the shifting perspective, here more strictly formalized, more deliberate than in any other O'Hara fiction. Although the bulk of the story is related in O'Hara's familiar omniscient voice, the author employs a first-person narrator to illuminate and intensify the tale. The story focuses largely upon Robert Millhouser, yet by opening and closing with the narrator, Gerald Higgins, the writer makes the lives of the two so conjoin that at the novel's end one has seen into the histories of *both men,* learning about each through the other. Moreover, by means of this strategy O'Hara also reinforces his theme, basic to his entire world-view. This theme, stated syllogistically, is that (a) learning about others demands involvement with them; (b) in this process one inevitably learns about one's self; (c) as one's self-knowledge broadens and deepens, the more aware one becomes of mankind's common fates and failures. Yet, this humanistic and affirmative thesis must be measured against another, starker proposition also advanced by the novel and recurrent in O'Hara's work: that one can glimpse only fleetingly into the mysteries of the heart.

O'Hara's method in *Ourselves to Know* utilizes a third device, alternation in time, which involves the flashback, the pre-view (or foreshadowing), and what might be termed the simultaneous moment. The narrative voice of *Ourselves to Know* is that of Gerald Higgins, who tells the story twenty years after he first wrote it; but the narrative itself is cast largely in the present tense because it purports to depict events at the time of their occurrence. Further, within the narrative there are shifts in the time order, either to divulge later events or to recall others past. Although this device of story within a story is potentially far more complex than O'Hara's actual handling of it (Faulkner, for example, practices a similar method, but more as a function of his angle of vision than as a device), there are instances in the novel when O'Hara achieves the startling effect of simultaneity in depth. This effect is analogous to that one gets in playing multi-dimensional chess, or by looking at one's reflection in a mirror while holding another mirror in which is reflected one's image, and so on *ad infinitum.*

As a consequence of these various techniques, this novel is far more carefully proportioned and incomparably more selective than *From the Terrace;* it absorbs the reader far more intensely than the previous book despite its lesser action. The focus of *Ourselves to Know* narrows upon the protagonist's twenties and thirties and the two years of his marriage and tells almost nothing of his teens, his early middle age, or the thirty-six years between his wife's death and his own. Nevertheless, by the time the reader has arrived at the novel's conclusion, he has witnessed the complete cycle of events and perceived the factors comprising the characters' motivations. The result is a satisfying sense of both the writer's control and his work's intricate architecture. The novel is further unified by the constancy of its focus upon a few highly specific locales in the O'Hara country, mainly Lyons and Fort Penn.[16]

The book's title drawn from a line in Pope's "Essay on Man," suggests its major theme: "And all our Knowledge is, ourselves to know." As Millhouser says to Higgins, in a passage of the sort persistently recurrent in O'Hara's novels: "How often we are mistaken! We think we know one man very well, and something happens that shows us we didn't know him at all. That's the sort of thing that happens in many close friendships. Think how often it happens in our relations with men and women who are *not* our close friends. That's when you realize how little we know of our fellow man. Who knows me? Who on earth knows me?"[17] And, if the novel offers a resolution to this dilemma, it is that man must, regardless of the outcome and because his very nature so demands, seek to know himself and his fellows and somehow manage to live with that knowledge—as does Robert Millhouser. His conduct serves as a parable. Instead of taking up another, easier identity elsewhere and enjoying his comfortable fortune and still vigorous health, Millhouser returns to Lyons, Pennsylvania, where he has killed his wife. There he lives out his remaining thirty-six years, attends to his affairs, and faces his hostile townsmen each day; and at night he sleeps (?) in the room, the very bed, in which he had committed the murder. One can only infer what torment Millhouser endures in privacy. His friend, Ben Rosebery, calls this life "an elegant prison"; Millhouser corrects him and names it instead "a comfortable monastery" (403). It is left to the reader to determine which it is— or what else it might be.

When Gerald Higgins, the amanuensis, tries to make Millhouser talk about those years, Millhouser refuses, fending Higgins off with oblique and cryptic replies. Instead of answering him with reasoned certainties, Millhouser quotes to Higgins a composite passage from Meredith's poem "Modern Love":

> Then each applied to each that fatal knife,
> Deep questioning, which probes to endless dole.
> Ah, what a dusty answer gets the soul
> When hot for certainties in this our life!—
> No villain need be! Passions spin the plot:
> We are betrayed by what is false within (406-7).

And with the utmost feeling he responds to Higgins queries: "We *mustn't* expect the absolute answers!" (407). Accordingly, Millhouser's penultimate remark to Higgins is that he has exposed to Higgins only certain parts of his life, a statement which casts doubt on the reliability of the entire history Higgins has composed (the history being read) and also emphasizes O'Hara's conviction that the whole truth of man's nature and experience ultimately defies his grasp and comprehension. In this instance at least, O'Hara's belief rests upon the authority of a subtle, provocative, and skillfully crafted novel. Any ambiguity in substance derives from the complexities of the theme itself, not from the defects of its vehicle.

A second and related theme advanced by *Ourselves to Know* is suggested by yet another quotation, one from Milton's *Paradise Regained*, which Millhouser discovers in prison while he awaits trial for murder. To Millhouser these lines describe his condition, his sense of numbness and loss of all human feeling: "All hope is lost/Of my reception into grace; what worse?/For where no hope is left, is left no fear" (385). And Millhouser's discovery and contemplation of these lines is swiftly followed by his conclusion that Hope is the most precious of all Graces.

At this point the question intrudes itself, if only to veteran members of O'Hara's audience, whether O'Hara himself considers a state of numbness or stoicism desirable. Many hostile readers, taking at face value O'Hara's seeming objectivity and detachment, view his apparent lack of feeling as one of his great defects. They find him simply "cold." Yet has not this reaction always been one of the contemporary reader's standard responses to the Realist-Naturalist of his day? Likewise, O'Hara's stoicism and dispassion is both a method which permits him wider freedom in the selection and presentation of his material, and a defense mechanism, a necessary pose, reminiscent of the legendary old Negro's. Asked why he always sang and laughed despite the harshness of his existence, the Negro replied that it was either sing and laugh or cut his throat. The very depth and intensity of O'Hara's feeling demand that it be masked, contained, channeled; broached, it might flood out the reader and the narrative.

To translate O'Hara's attitudes into the terms of his novel, one must now understand that the novelist's position is like that of Robert Millhouser. Millhouser confesses to Ben Rosebery that, by killing his wife, he has destroyed his own capacity for feeling, a condition he finds dreadful; and he later tells Gerald Higgins in their final meeting, when the facts of the story have been exposed, that one does not worship God by praying for the repression of man's natural spirit, for the spirit itself is a divine creation. From this statement it can also be inferred, in reply to Higgins' question, that sometime during the years following his wife's death Millhouser *did* return to life, however crippled. His friendship and collaboration with Higgins, and his concern that the story be recorded for others to see (and so that Higgins himself might find instruction in it), comprise irrefutable evidence of Millhouser's re-identification with the world of men; it also conveys the implicit evidence of O'Hara's own toughminded optimism. Had Millhouser's story been only an apology, a self-justification, his telling it would constitute no such evidence of regained identification; but the recital makes no effort to spare himself or to defend his criminal act. Rather, it conveys the record of how deeply men can feel, even such seemingly reserved and cold men as Robert Millhouser, and to what extremes their passions can drive them. "Passions spin the plot."

When Millhouser kills Hedda, he does so upon greater provocation than her infidelity. Not only has she cuckolded him with a man by far his inferior, but so shamelessly and brazenly it becomes public scandal, eventually returning to him. Moreover, when he questions Hedda, she flaunts her infidelities, seduces him into making love to her, and in the process renders him impotent by her cold matter-of-factness. This sexual incapacity, which she has induced, deals the final humiliation to his pride as a man; his humiliation, more than any notion of outraged morality, causes him to pull the trigger soon afterward.

Many reviewers of the novel questioned Robert's motivation and queried why he should later commit murder when he knows from the start what sort of female his wife is. Such criticism, however, betrays an unreflective reading of the book. At the beginning of his marriage Robert had indeed known he was too old and Hedda too fickle for him to hold her favor. Wisely, he had resolved to enjoy her youthful passion and beauty only so long as he could, then to let her go, and to give her in return for this brightening of his lonely middle age the comfort, power, and respectability of the Millhouser name and wealth. But his feeling for her grew too deep, and her manner of betraying him and her complete contempt for his feelings conjoined to overpower his reason, just as the emotions of O'Hara's characters frequently overpower their logic and wills. Millhouser had not been able to perform the overreaching act of love and forgiveness which is somehow the choice of O'Hara's protagonists at the crisis in their lives.

Hedda, source of Millhouser's most ecstatic happiness and excruciating misery, is another of O'Hara's destructive women: a demonic, beautiful, driven, doomed creature of the senses, she is irresistible in her allure. Childlike and yet ageless in her wisdom, she manifests the irrefragable realities of the flesh. Like O'Hara's passionate women, her sexuality, once aroused, is stronger and more urgent than that of any male; indeed, it uses the male to its own purposes. The reader knows little about her becoming; he only knows how she is. But, in this instance, O'Hara's treatment is persuasive enough that the fact of her nature tends to loom larger than any question about its formation.

Other than the necessary treatment of sexuality as it affects the destiny of Robert Millhouser, it is not a prime concern in *Ourselves to Know*. It enters significantly into only one other important aspect of the story, and then obliquely. Millhouser's history, poignant for its own sake, takes on additional import when one learns in the novel's concluding line that Higgins too, sixteen years after setting down Millhouser's biography, finds himself in a similar predicament: cuckolded. O'Hara offers no details of Higgins' response and only a hint of the mental torture he must have undergone, but to all appearances Higgins has learned something from Millhouser because he writes as though he and his wife still live together in a functioning marriage. Ironically, Higgins may have fulfilled the prophecy implicit in Millhouser's parting remark to him, many years earlier: "Look out, Gerald. You may find what you're looking for. Yourself" (408).

The lack of preoccupation with matters which have elsewhere concerned O'Hara almost to obsession—social class, the power of money, cultural history—is one of the several distinctions of *Ourselves to Know*. Unquestionably representative of O'Hara's mature work, its discipline, originality, and wholeness of conception demand that it be ranked with *Appointment in Samarra* and with *Ten North Frederick* as one of the author's superior fictions. Less vividly written, perhaps, than *A Rage to Live, Ourselves to Know* is more durably constructed, subtler, more profound. In its own quiet way it insists upon recognition as a memorable and skillfully executed work.

VI Elizabeth Appleton: *The Method of Ironic Contrast*

John O'Hara's most recent novel appears to be a kind of mutation. Although set somewhere in the O'Hara country, it could as easily and credibly take place in any Eastern college town; the characters, a college dean, his wife, assorted academics, and a few townspeople, seem hardly typical of the usual O'Hara cast. Moreover, the situation, hinging upon the selection of a new president for Spring Valley College, does not seem the sort to be of concern to O'Hara. There also hovers about the tale an aura of sentiment quite untypical of its ordinarily dispassionate author. However, further reflection upon the book quickly dispels these misleading surmises, and the trained reader soon discovers in it hidden dimensions of craft and theme.

First, the novel's tight structure depends upon characteristic O'Hara strategies. Among its fundamental structural devices is suspended time, with Chapter I set in the story's present moment —the interval just preceding its climactic issue: will John Appleton be elected to the presidency of the college he has served well as professor and as dean, thus fulfilling the ambitions of his beautiful and aristocratic wife Elizabeth? True to his fashion, O'Hara reveals the answer at the end of the same chapter: that John Appleton will *not* be so honored. Likewise true to his fashion, O'Hara has also surrounded the issue with such a host of portentous relationships, complex emotions, and intriguing characters that the reader's curiosity about the issue itself becomes subordinated to the desire to know *all* about this superficially sedate college town.

Accordingly, the technique of suspending time opens the way for O'Hara to reconstruct the events, attitudes, and emotions which engendered the present moment. Beginning with the next chapter, O'Hara returns to the past, to the first meeting of John and Elizabeth Appleton almost twenty years earlier; and in each succeeding chapter he broaches the significant episodes in their lives and introduces other crucial characters, bringing us at last, in the novel's final chapter, to the exact moment at which Chapter I had ended. In this instance, O'Hara's method adheres closely to the flashback technique; that is, all action between the novel's opening and closing chapters occurs in the past, with the past arranged in its proper chronological order as it marches steadily toward the present. O'Hara's time-sense in *Elizabeth Appleton* is linear rather than circular as in *Ourselves to Know*.

Within this overall pattern there are other familiar O'Hara methods at work, although often in new combinations and with varied application. For example, the technique of shifting perspectives which was first so impressively employed in *Appointment in Samarra* once more comes into play. Skillfully shifting both his focus and his narrative approach, and varying the construction of each chapter, O'Hara achieves an effect of change and fluctuation which forestalls the tedium elsewhere damaging to the later sections of *A Rage to Live* and to much of *From the Terrace*. A number of chapters in *Elizabeth Appleton* are thus comprised largely of narration and description; others make use of a single extended dramatic scene; some are a combination of the panoramic and scenic; and yet others are composed of several separate but related scenes.

Indeed, one of the most remarkable aspects of this unpretentious and low-keyed novel is its expertise. In the hands of a less practiced artisan, the story could easily have degenerated into soap-opera. One notes, for example, that the first ninety-five pages of *Elizabeth Appleton* are almost entirely dramatic in construction. The author's voice is rarely heard; the reader learns by watching the characters in action and by listening to them.

Considering O'Hara's special skill at dramatic scene and dialogue, the effect attained is that of strong psychological realism. Much of the novel is similarly devised, so that not until the last hundred pages does one find sections of narration and description. As a result of this consistently dramatic technique, the novel moves very swiftly. Despite its standard length, it reads like a *novella;* and, significantly, it flags momentarily only at the two-thirds mark, where narration-description begins to supplant dramatic scene, although O'Hara recovers completely with two vivid, rapidly paced closing chapters.

Of further significance is the fact that the structural design of the novel accurately reflects its thematic concerns. Two thirds of *Elizabeth Appleton* deals with love and marriage; and, although these subjects remain pertinent, the romantic factor definitely becomes subsidiary to the quest for the college presidency which dominates the novel's final phase. If the presidency can be held to represent social status, the novel is thus proportioned with remarkable fidelity to O'Hara's fundamental interests. Other than the relationship between men and women as lovers or as marriage partners, O'Hara's attention is also given in passing, with commendable restraint, to such social matters as the college's image in the minds of its alumni, the effect one's background and manners has on professional advancement (the Jewish professor burdened additionally by his noisy, pushy wife), and the subtle dominance Elizabeth can exert over the college community by means of her social graces and the awe inspired by her rumored wealth.

But O'Hara's craft in *Elizabeth Appleton* does not confine itself to the novel's architecture and thematic symmetry. He also creates one of his more memorable characters in Elizabeth Appleton, delineating her by means of an ingenious method of ironic contrast so unobtrusive it needs careful study to be appreciated.

By casting Elizabeth as the central figure of the novel, from whom all other characters and major events radiate, O'Hara makes her the story's "heroine" for the unsuspecting reader. That is, the reader tends to take her as worthy and admirable, as well as important. Yet is she admirable? One finds even such usually sophisticated observers as Gore Vidal snared in the traditional notion that a novel's central character must also be its "hero" or spokesman.[18] Hardly. In one of the more cunning performances in recent fiction, O'Hara has portrayed a heroine (a protagonist, really) who at best only partly deserves sympathy and admiration and who at worst deserves condemnation. To put the case emphatically, a sizeable part of O'Hara's audience, including some critics who should have known better, entirely missed the author's *sotto voce* but pervasive irony; they accepted at face value a character whose words, actions, and motives demand the most careful and skeptical appraisal.

Indeed, the salient instance in which Elizabeth's version of reality may differ from the facts requires attention. In a number of the novel's most vivid scenes, Elizabeth delivers a derogatory, even contemptuous, assessment of her husband's quality as a man. This attitude is implied in the first chapter when she implicitly accuses John Appleton of harboring sexual feelings for her sister; it is emphasized at the end of Chapter II when she first deceives her husband by spending money given her by her mother and not telling him about it, then concludes that "it was not hard to keep from him things he did not want to know."[19] This attitude is also treated as it pertains to their sexual relationship when Elizabeth artfully deludes her husband by the feigned passion of her caresses (her true feelings are now directed toward a lover) and contents herself with the same conclusion: "that John Appleton was a master at self-deception" (147). A few pages later Elizabeth, in the course of discussing her husband's weaknesses with her lover, asserts that her husband's ego could never withstand a divorce, that "he'd collapse like a toy balloon," perhaps even commit suicide (156). Finally, just before the novel ends, Elizabeth says of John (this time to her sister): "He has no real guts, and he isn't all that intellectual, either" (299).

Considering that Elizabeth was presumably once in love with John Appleton and that she intends to remain married to him despite her contempt, it might be instructive to examine him carefully and to place his words and deeds in apposition to his wife's judgment. First, John Appleton comes of sound family, with ancestors who have been clergymen and teachers. He himself has graduated from the college he now serves as dean; as a student, he worked to pay his own expenses and distinguished himself in three varsity sports, yet maintained grades sufficient for admission to graduate work at Harvard. After graduate school, he returns to Spring Valley as a teacher of history, becomes one of the campus's most respected professors, rises rapidly to a deanship, and would have been the college's president but for the quirky behavior of the trustees. Meanwhile, he has seen combat duty in the navy and won promotion to lieutenant commander.

The external evidence, therefore, does not at once seem to support Elizabeth's concept of her husband as a man so weak he would be crushed by his wife's departure. Nor is there anywhere support for Elizabeth's conclusion that her husband needs constant praise and ego-support because he lacked affection from his father. His activities derive either from his natural inclinations and talents or from necessity. The deanship he accepts because it is thrust upon him; the presidency was from the start his wife's ambition rather than his own. In any case, his career bears little resemblance to that of the whining, self-pitying, narcissistic, and emotionally alienated potential suicide. Certainly his conduct in the most disappointing event of his life, his loss of the college presidency to an inferior man, could not be more sportsmanlike and manly, whatever he may have felt inwardly.

But none of these facts necessarily refutes Elizabeth's charges that John is weak and self-deceiving. Of the self-deception we should note that her conclusion derives largely from her success as a liar and adulteress. Because she manages to keep her husband from learning about the disposal of both her extra funds and extra favors, she determines that he *wishes* to be fooled and is thus weak. Her reasoning exactly parallels that of the temporarily successful criminal who goes free to enjoy the spoils of his misdeeds while despising the police for allowing him his freedom. In fact, only one episode in the novel could possibly be construed as illustrative of John's weakness: the instance in which he later qualifies in a public letter a slighting reference, made during a classroom lecture, to one of the college's chief benefactors (also the town's leading millionaire). However, the reflective reader perceives that this, too, operates to John's credit; for he behaves as a man who seeks to amend an earlier, irresponsible act. That he does not eat "humble pie" is quite evident from the continued hostility of an influential trustee that later affects John's candidacy for the president's chair.

As to Elizabeth's deception of her husband regarding money and sexual fidelity, his deportment can be explained by other modes of logic than hers. Although John *knows* that his wife receives large cash gifts from her mother and uses them to provide benefits his salary could not encompass, he does not believe this expenditure to be a matter for contention. He has confidence in the strength of his marriage; he feels himself to be master in his home; and he loves Elizabeth to the degree that he wishes to indulge her in some things (she seems never to understand this). Her money, moreover, is disbursed intelligently for such expenses as a second car and the children's education.

Similarly, Elizabeth's efficiency in conducting an illicit romance without her husband's suspicion depends upon other factors than John's gullibility. Most of her affair with Porter Ditson takes place while John is away at war; moreover, Elizabeth herself plans matters with the greatest caution and discretion, which includes the continued delusion of her husband through consummate bedroom performances with him before he leaves for military service. How, then, should he know that his wife no longer finds him her romantic hero?

Elizabeth Appleton's cruel assessment of her husband can now be viewed for what it is: a creation of her own needs and imagination, and a construct which implicitly discredits her far more than him. For, regardless of Elizabeth's beauty and charm, and despite the suffering she undergoes late in the narrative—a suffering which may tempt the tenderhearted reader into forgiveness and renewed admiration—she emerges as the most recent in the line of O'Hara's destructive females; she is a woman whose desires brook no interference. The only two men who approach an understanding of her are her father (whom she hates and who warns John never to let her get the upper hand), and her lover Porter Ditson, whom she badly scars despite his awareness of the sharpness of her talons. As he tells her just before she ends their affair: "...love isn't the thing with you any more, Elizabeth. As a matter of fact...it never really was... when you married John Appleton, you were going by an instinct. You knew that marrying him was a surer way of getting what you wanted than if you'd married...someone like me...my love for you isn't only sex, and yours for me very nearly is" (249-50). And so she leaves her lover impaired by having demanded from him just the sort of emotional commitment he had always avoided for his own self-preservation. But she does not escape unmarked. The end of her affair also signals the end of her youth; thereafter she carries within herself "instead of guilt and fear . . . a benign deadness . . . And pity" (300).

We have ascertained that Elizabeth is capable of lying, deception, and adultery. What else? Snobbery, especially cruel to those who are timid and insecure because Elizabeth exudes it unconsciously; it has been bred into her. While her background of money, fashionable schools, and aristocratic friends has given her poise and charm, it has also endowed her with a manner deadly to those of whom she disapproves. From the one close inspection O'Hara allows the reader of the Appleton children, it also appears certain that under his mother's aegis at least the son will grow into an insufferable snob, wholly unlike his democratic father.

As has been earlier implied, O'Hara does not intend to make his protagonist a monster. She is no Mary Eaton. His attitude toward her is ambivalent. Thus, as the novel concludes, she attempts an honest self-evaluation and asserts her willingness to withstand the consequences of her own acts, but does not undergo any moral regeneration. Indeed, moral values are absent from her thinking and her makeup, as they are generally lacking in O'Hara's women. (The men in O'Hara's work think morally about what should be; the women think about what they want.) She neither glorifies her misdeeds nor exalts her motives for them, but she recognizes the limitations in her affair with Ditson and confesses to herself that the basis of her admiration and affection for her former lover was primarily sexual.

Perhaps Elizabeth's most inspiring and simultaneously incongruous facet of character is her attitude toward marriage, for in the novel's terminal chapter O'Hara indicates to the attentive reader that Elizabeth has been permitted a partial return from damnation, even into purgatory, by making her the spokesman for what is undoubtedly his own view of marriage. In a dialogue with her twice-divorced sister, Elizabeth avows: "You can't ever be sure . . . The only way you can be sure is if you make up your mind you're going to stay married no matter what happens. Cruelty. Infidelity. Drinking. Temperamental differences. And even then you can only speak for yourself" (290). Later, continuing the dialogue, Elizabeth says: "I don't believe in divorce when the only reason for it is wanting to sleep with someone else"; she then adds: "a happy marriage, the kind that you're looking for, is an absurd, foolish dream. So stop looking for it." (297-98). And as a final statement she asserts: "Romantic love and sexual curiosity haven't been part of our marriage for years and years. But I'm his wife, and that's how he thinks of me, habitually. I've hated him sometimes, and I'm sure he's hated me.... But we're a marriage ... I have found out that I could give up a happy, exciting relationship with the only man I ever loved, and go back to the only one I ever married" (299).

These comments have a special edge honed by Elizabeth's recent past, but they are no less penetrating because of it. Considering what she has lived and in view of her thoughts about marriage, her husband's remarks as the book ends take on a keen irony. In jest, but with a far different sort of truth than he realizes, John Appleton says to the sisters: "it doesn't pay to have any secrets from your husband," and a moment later, with even sharper unwitting irony, he tells them: "The Webster girls make good wives" (309-10).

Throughout the novel, and most notably in the characterization of its protagonist, one perceives again O'Hara's conviction that the female of the species is better fitted for survival than the male. Not only are the men less able to withstand continued emotional stress, as Jarvis Webster (Elizabeth's father) is more deeply disturbed than his wife by the death of their son—although she was partly responsible for it—and as Porter Ditson's entire life-style is affected by his affair with Elizabeth, but they are inferior in other ways. Furthermore, the women tend to outlive their husbands, inheriting their estates and so gaining control of material means for the expression of their natural superiority. They are tougher and shrewder than the men in worldly affairs: Elizabeth, not John, wants the college presidency and impels him toward it; Barbara Speacht becomes the brains for Bruce McAndrews and formulates exactly the right strategy to keep John Appleton from succeeding McAndrews; Evangeline Ditson's brains and money loom behind Brice Ditson, and so on. The women of Spring Valley, Pennsylvania, as elsewhere in the O'Hara country, are also more animalistic than the men, especially in their sexual drives and appetites. In his persuasive demonstration of this in *Elizabeth Appleton*, O'Hara has reworked one of his major themes with originality and skill.

VII *Pennsylvania in the Shorter Fiction*

O'Hara's use of Gibbsville and Pennsylvania settings in his
shorter fiction parallels the employment of these locales in his
novels, at least in one obvious way: except for a very few early
stories contemporaneous with *Appointment in Samarra*, O'Hara
did not return to Pennsylvania for his story backgrounds until
the latter half of his career. However, beginning with *The Farmer's Hotel* (1951), O'Hara has made frequent trips back to his
imagined country, and mined its apparently inexhaustible ores
with consistent success in a number of praiseworthy *novellas*
and stories, some representative instances of which deserve
comment.

Although the dust jacket and title page of *The Farmer's Hotel*
describe it as a novel, it is, in fact, a *novella*. And a tight piece
of work it is: expertly crafted, carefully conceived, convincingly
cast. Furthermore, beneath its surface action one perceives the
themes of a serious, provocative allegory.

As his tale's foundation O'Hara utilizes the classic situation of
travelers at an inn, brought together by circumstances (in this
instance a fierce snowstorm), who for a few hours enjoy a
peculiar intimacy and candor. Instead of passing the time by
telling stories, they reveal some of the truths about themselves
and entertain one another with good food, drink, and songs.
The one disturbing element is a foulmouthed, bullying truck-
driver, whose brutish conduct first disrupts the festive and com-
radely atmosphere and later results in the murder of two of
those who had participated in it.

O'Hara has constructed the *novella* almost entirely in dramatic
terms; its three parts closely correspond to the functions of the
acts of a play: exposition, crisis, dénouement. The first part
establishes the setting and situation, identifies each of the eleven
characters participating directly in the action, and foreshadows
the final tragedy. The second part develops the inter-relationships
among the characters, stresses the camaraderie which springs up
despite their various backgrounds and temperaments, and ends
with the crisis forced by the brutal Rogg. Part Three is very
brief and serves as the resolution. The state trooper who in Part
One had urged the travelers to remain at the inn for the night
now returns to announce that Rogg has rammed his truck into

the car carrying the lovers Martha and Pomfret, and has killed them both.

The dramatic structure of *The Farmer's Hotel* is reinforced by its narrative method. Except for brief passages written in an unobtrusive omniscient mode, the story is cast entirely as dialogue. With very slight alteration it could be staged effectively (in its dramatic form, later included in O'Hara's volume of plays, it displays virtually no substantive difference). Furthermore, O'Hara handles the dialogue with exceeding sureness, delineating each character precisely and economically both by the manner and content of his speech. With the exception of some needlessly detailed passages concerning what the travelers eat at their impromptu banquet, the *novella* contains no slack. Its pace varies, sometimes swift sometimes leisurely, but always demonstrating the author's perfect control. The narrative begins slowly, builds in a rising action to the climax at the end of Part Two, and, then, after a brief, deceptively calm interlude, concludes powerfully with the shocking news of the two deaths.

Within this carefully structured framework, motivation and theme are evolved with admirable skill. At first each of the story's characters is immersed in his own special problems: Ira Studebaker frets about his new hotel and nourishes his still fresh grief for his wife recently dead of cancer; Pomfret and Martha struggle against the complications arising from their illicit love affair; Jerry and his girls labor under their tangled love and money worries; Rogg is preoccupied with his gambling activities. Moreover, each initially remains behind the wall of his own class behavior: the aloofness and arrogance of the aristocratic lovers, the bravado and wise-cracking of the show people, the profanity and braggardliness of the truckdriver. Then, as they begin to know one another and to depend upon one another's company for comfort against the blizzard outside and their own imminent cares, class lines blur and disintegrate. Soon they are all people together, hardly equal in strength or intelligence or talent or rank, but all alike in their humanity. Even Rogg is tolerable until the fundamental animality of his nature asserts itself in his coarse treatment of the girls and destroys the idyllic mood of all.

It seems clear that O'Hara intends this tale as an allegory, if not of man's universal condition at least of his life here and now. As has been suggested, the characters represent the various classes: the high, by Pomfret and Martha; the middle, by Ira, Dr. Graeff, and Mrs. Fenstermacher; the low, by Jerry, the Pickwick sisters, and Rogg. Charles, the Negro, occupies a special position: low, by virtue of his race and occupation; high, by virtue of his dignity, talent, and strength. The allegory can also be extended to include a cosmic element: the snowstorm partly responsible for the tragedy.

Of special significance within this allegorical framework is the character of Joe Rogg: big, tough, foul of mouth and thought, boastful, totally without regard for the feelings of others, and, as we finally learn, viciously capable of coldblooded murder. Withal, O'Hara makes him credible. Although we know nothing about Rogg's past, we infer from his conduct that he was reared in some concrete jungle. "Poor slob," Pomfret calls him, while Ira, most sanguine of the company (and among its most naïve members), says of Rogg: "He doesn't know any better." But, if Rogg's behavior can be partially excused as having been conditioned by improper environment, his final act of willful murder forbids any such permissive interpretation. His is an act of total depravity; and, in the O'Hara view of human nature—as we eventually recognize it—depravity, basic and irremediable, is indeed its source. Joe Rogg is finally explicable only as a "bad seed," one of those naturally and inherently evil men who can only be reformed, as Twain says of Pap Finn, with a shotgun.

To see O'Hara's allegory whole, with the characters of *The Farmer's Hotel* as representative of humanity, Joe Rogg thus becomes the Outlaw: a potential Attila, Capone, Hitler. So viewed, O'Hara's parable is explicit. Either the good men are strong and wise enough to control the outlaws by exerting superior force, or they give them their way and let them take what they wish. A third alternative would be to placate Rogg, to turn the other cheek and gentle him with meekness and all-forgiving love; but O'Hara suggests this possibility only faintly and with no conviction. What O'Hara unmistakably implies is that the Roggs of this planet most need killing, not forgiveness.

A Family Party (1956) exhibits O'Hara in a far mellower mood. Set in the small Pennsylvania town of Lyons (also the locale of *Ourselves to Know* and an occasional later short story), it is written in the form of a monologue. Although O'Hara often uses the monologue for satire or parody, in *A Family Party* he employs it to capture the special flavor and nostalgia of a testimonial dinner to a small-town physician after forty years of service. The monologue technique permits O'Hara to achieve a multiple effect. He can depict the subject of the speaker's remarks; he can by indirection characterize the speaker himself; he can also, by means of the distancing effect inherent in the monologue approach, introduce much emotion via the speaker without himself appearing sentimental. Thus a great deal is accomplished by implication, and the reader finds that he knows far more than the speaker has seemed to tell him.

For example, while high and undoubtedly deserved praise is given to Dr. Sam Merritt for his generosity, kindness, charity, and nobility of spirit, little is said about his professional ability. Only one episode indicates that he might have been anything more than adequate as a physician: when he performed an amputation with a saw, the only instrument available to him. In any case, he has won the respect and love of his townsmen because of his excellence as a man rather than for his professional expertise.

Although the monologue meanders along apparently in random and unpremeditated fashion, it actually hinges upon a number of pivotal events strategically placed. It opens with the speaker's description of Sam Merritt covered with gore and working frantically to save the lives of miners injured in a train wreck (as Dr. Patrick O'Hara once similarly labored). Later, the narrative suggests that Sam was motivated to practice medicine, against his natural inclination, by the death of an older brother of spinal meningitis. And the story closes with two delayed revelations: the first relating how Sam sacrificed his most precious personal ambition in order to advance the public welfare; the second recounting the deep agony borne by him privately because of the insanity of his beloved wife. Coming as they do hard upon one another at the end of the story, these two revelations intensify and heighten its effect. What has been a pleasantly nostalgic but not especially urgent tale suddenly becomes poignant and memorable at the exposure of the hidden misery of this admirable man.

Finally, the reader surmises from this modest work some of O'Hara's great affection and admiration for his father, who, like Sam Merritt, was a doctor in a small Pennsylvania city. Although we gather that Dr. O'Hara was far more professionally distinguished than the hero of *A Family Party,* the writer has nevertheless set forth in his fictional creation many of the qualities of character which must have been exemplified by his own father, as in other men of the same calling. Certainly this passage could stand as a tribute to all: "Old or young, rich or poor, we all felt better for having Sam in charge because we had the confidence that with Sam there beside us and looking after us, we had more than a doctor there. We had if not a friend—those that did not know him on that basis—we had the instinctive feeling that here was a man that the thing he wanted most in the world was for us to get well, and if there was anything in his power, he'd see to it that he did." Another part of that tribute resides in these words, spoken earlier, revealing O'Hara in an unusually affirmative and idealistic vein: "A doctor is always righting wrong. That's his business, or profession, if you prefer. He is supposed to cure people, which is the same thing as righting wrong."[20]

The elements of nostalgia, recollection, character portraiture and moral conviction so prominently displayed in *A Family Party* are also manifest in the increasing number of stories with Pennsylvania or Gibbsville settings which have appeared among O'Hara's collections of recent years. Because O'Hara's memory for the scenes of his youth obviously has sharpened with time and distance, these Pennsylvania tales stand out in their frequency and length and in the special mood and attitude they convey.

Many of these stories could well be gathered and accurately described under the title *The Way It Was*. That is, one of O'Hara's prime inspirations for this phase of his work is the urge to record a kind of personal history of the time, place, and quality of his own youth. We recall his open declaration of that intention. Thus in such pieces as "Ninety Minutes Away" and "Exterior with Figure" (in *The Hat on the Bed* [1964]) or "Claude Emerson, Reporter" and "Winter Dance" (in *The Cape Cod Lighter* [1962]) one suspects that, whatever the individual story's intention or focus, O'Hara's dominant impulse is autobiographical. Quite aside from such clues as the Gibbsville or Lyons locale and the presence of an O'Hara surrogate like Malloy or Higgins, the work itself often has the texture of a memoir. Some, like "Winter Dance," can only be explained as autobiography, focusing as they do so intensely on mood and milieu. Yet others, like "The Engineer" (*The Cape Cod Lighter*), "A Case

History" (*Assembly* [1961]) and "Claude Emerson, Reporter" are
essentially extended vignettes or fictional biographies. Moreover,
while the writing in them is uniformly polished and while they
frequently convey some illuminating insight into human nature
or an instructive moral lesson, they sometimes share in the major
defect of the novels in their predilection for the historical rather
than for the fictive or dramatic.

This imperfection must, however, be measured against O'Hara's
very substantial achievement in his Pennsylvania stories; for,
true to the generality of O'Hara's recent short fiction, they
demonstrate a degree and frequency of excellence rarely sur-
passed by other story writers now at work. Such pieces as "The
Man on the Tractor" (*The Hat on the Bed*), "Pat Collins" (*The
Cape Cod Lighter*) and "The Cellar Domain" (*Assembly*)—each
with a Gibbsville setting—not only show O'Hara at his best but
also how varied his best can be. A brief analysis of the last of
these stories will perhaps serve to document this point.

In "The Cellar Domain" O'Hara takes such unpretentious
material as a Gibbsville barbershop and creates from it a complex mosaic depicting the interfusion of human feelings and
social protocols. Peter Durant conducts his barber shop as a
benevolent despot, catering only to Gibbsville's most important men. But when the business is threatened by the patronage
of Andy McKeever, a jovial, vulgar fellow whom Peter likes but
who is of decidedly lower caste than the shop's other customers,
the proprietor faces a difficult decision: should he continue
to serve Andy according to his own whim and authority as the
proprietor, or should he please his other customers by turning
Andy away to retain the prestige and "toniness" of his trade?
Peter chooses the first alternative, maintaining his personal
integrity; but he pays for his choice in the destruction of other
oldtime loyalties and alliances with both his employees and
his customers.

Whatever else the story illustrates, it discloses how a once
good, wise man has become a petty tyrant, corrupted by the
exercise of authority too long unchallenged. As is frequently
the case in O'Hara, moral decision does not take place in a
vacuum. Tough-minded Realist that he is, he demonstrates in
"The Cellar Domain" as elsewhere that a seemingly good act
may have evil consequences, or that a good deed may be done
for the wrong reasons, or that what may be justice for one often

constitutes injustice for another. Were O'Hara a more explicitly political or philosophical writer, one would unhesitatingly read this story as allegory and apply it to such wide-ranging issues as totalitarianism, racial integration, property rights, individual freedoms and responsibilities, and proper social behavior. The reader can make these interpolations for himself if he wishes; in the process, he may perhaps remind himself in wonder from time to time that this is the work of a writer in disfavor with the majority of academic critics because he produces supposedly flimsy, popular, superficial stuff.

Appointment in Samarra, Ten North Frederick, Ourselves to Know—flimsy, popular, superficial? Surely the terrain encompassed in these and other fictions of the O'Hara country is large and significant enough to merit some other, less invidious adjectives. Surely we must make room for them and their imagined world on literary maps. Without O'Hara's Pennsylvania stories and novels how much less Americans would know about a segment of their landscape; and how much less they would know about those areas of experience which O'Hara has charted with greater craft than anyone now writing in the United States.

CHAPTER 4

New York and Hollywood

I N O'HARA'S SECOND NOVEL *Butterfield 8* (1935) there
appears a character named Jimmy Malloy whose personality
encompasses a series of contradictory traits. A hard-drinking
young man eager for fun and the company of beautiful women,
his surface belligerence and cynical wise-cracking barely disguise his great sentimentality and capacity for tenderness. He
dresses carefully in Brooks clothes and soft white buttoned-
down shirts; at the same time, he never forgets his identity
as a "Mick," a rebel who declares that he will never aspire to
membership in the upper classes because he had not long before
been saved from starvation and complete despondency only
through the kindness of a Negro janitress.

Although Malloy enjoys his status as a newspaperman, he is in
imminent danger of dismissal because a date with a pretty girl or
his own highly charged nerves can cause him to miss an assignment ("when I get excited on a story I usually get stewed").
He considers himself a writer but cannot discipline himself to
the assiduous collecting of facts necessary for capable reporting.
"I'm the kind of reporter that wants to be a dramatic critic,"
he says.[1] However, his deeper ambitions are already taking form:
he has sold a number of sketches to the *New Yorker* and a novel
is well under way. A small-town boy not long in the big city,
he has quickly accumulated an amazing knowledge of the celebrities, the mobsters, the film and stage people, the glamorous
rich, the politicians, and the other types who populate the
speakeasies and who give one kind of Manhattan life its special
quality. Part righteous moralist, part emancipated playboy,
both observer and participant, simultaneously hack and artist,
Jimmy Malloy is alternately enthralled and disgusted by the
spectacle around him.

No great imagination is required to perceive that the Jimmy Malloy of *Butterfield 8* is, in truth, the young John O'Hara. Whether or not the details set forth in the novel coincide exactly with the facts of O'Hara's life during this period, we have O'Hara's fictional counterpart in Malloy and in *Butterfield 8* the first extended treatment of that terrain which, together with Hollywood, constitutes the other half of the O'Hara country. Less credibly populated than his eastern Pennsylvania homeland and portrayed with less artistic success, the New York-Hollywood world has nevertheless fascinated O'Hara since early in his career. Furthermore, through the Malloy who partakes of this world, O'Hara enters as a character into his own fiction with far greater frequency than in the Pennsylvania novels and stories.

The action of *Butterfield 8* takes place in the spring of 1930, when O'Hara had already been in New York for more than two years. For several adventurous months after O'Hara left home and after he failed to find work with newspapers in Montana (where he had gone in pursuit of a young lady from Pottsville) and in Chicago, he supported himself precariously in a variety of jobs, including a tour as hand on a transatlantic ship. He came to New York late in 1927 and found employment with the help of Franklin P. Adams, to whose column "The Conning Tower" he had contributed several items while still a reporter in Pottsville and in Tamaqua. For the next several years O'Hara held a succession of positions: night rewrite man for the New York *Daily Mirror*, radio columnist (under the pen-name of "Franey Delaney") and movie critic for the *Morning Telegraph*, staff member of *Time*, reporter for the *Herald Tribune*, secretary to Heywood Broun, public relations man, managing editor of the *Pittsburgh Bulletin-Index*, and press agent for Warner Brothers.

O'Hara's tenure in most of these situations was brief because his personality clashed with that of one of his superiors or because his social life interrupted his regular and punctual attendance at his work. According to his close friend Wolcott Gibbs, O'Hara was dismissed from *Time* by Henry R. Luce with the comment that the magazine "had no use for a man who lolled in bed after nine o'clock in the morning." His employer in the public relations job recalls: "When O'Hara worked for me it was like Thomas Wolfe stopping off and being a stevedore for three days. You don't fire O'Hara; those fellows just dissolve."

However, Charles Einfeld, O'Hara's publicity chief at Warner Brothers, remembers O'Hara's performance with words of high praise: "He'd never written an ad in his life, but he wrote the damnedest ones you've ever seen. They were offbeat, provocative and great." This hectic period also included a two-year interval during which O'Hara was married to a young actress, Helen Pettit, from whom he was divorced in 1933.[2]

O'Hara's association with Hollywood began in 1934, when the promise exhibited by *Appointment in Samarra* won him a contract as film writer even before the novel's publication.[3] The association continued throughout the 1930's and early 1940's; and, although O'Hara drew much of his income from his film work, he nevertheless remained active as a fiction writer and kept his permanent residence in New York. Undoubtedly the temptations to commit himself completely to the movie work were great. By his own admission he was once paid as much as three thousand dollars a week, and he has said that he was offered opportunities which would have made him a millionaire; but, despite the conviviality and munificence of his Hollywood experience, it undoubtedly imposed conditions which he found highly distasteful as an artist and as a man. Therefore, while his film writing may have cost him time and energy, he never regarded it as more than a way of earning a living—which is not the same as accepting it as a way of life.[4] Certainly his capacity for moral judgment remained unimpaired during his Hollywood years; and, in his involvement in the very different mode of existence of New York and Hollywood, the boy from Pottsville, Pennsylvania, found abundant material for his applied researches into people of a special sort and into their milieu. This environment also became the basis for much of the social history which John O'Hara has declared to be his major concern.

I Butterfield 8: *The Demise of Flaming Youth*

On June 8, 1931, the body of a young woman was found washed up on the shore at Long Beach, Long Island. She was quickly identified as Starr Faithfull, stepdaughter of a retired chemist living at a fashionable address just two doors from that of the mayor of New York. At first characterized by her stepfather as an innocent girl with few friends and virtually no social experience, subsequent investigation conducted into the background of the presumably murdered girl disclosed quite another tale. Not only was she a well-known habitué of the speakeasies in New York; her conduct during a visit to London had provoked a minor scandal.

During the weeks following the girl's death, the Starr Faithfull case continued to be the subject of front-page stories in New York papers, with one revelation after another. She had been briefly treated for alcoholism at Bellevue, had earlier undergone psychiatric care at a private sanitarium, had engaged in a succession of amours, including some with men from the highest social circles, and had recorded many of her activities in lurid diaries. It was also learned that in her teens she had been debauched by an older man, a prominent Bostonian, who had agreed to a settlement of twenty thousand dollars as reimbursement to her parents for medical and psychiatric care necessitated by the episode. Finally, when the police discovered three suicide notes written to a ship's surgeon with whom she had been infatuated, the investigation was eventually dropped despite the protests of her stepfather, whose behavior and circumstances can only be described as "shady."[5]

Whether or not O'Hara himself knew a Starr Faithfull, her case undoubtedly provided the model for Gloria Wandrous of *Butterfield* 8. He declares in his novel that he does not intend her as a symbol for the flaming youth of her generation; nevertheless, she seems representative of the Speakeasy Era, the early years of the Depression when innocence, beauty, and youth could no longer be contained in the same vessel. The beginnings of despair had set in, and the abandon manifest both in the life of Starr Faithfull and in that of her fictional counterpart Gloria Wandrous were somehow right for the time. We can even make of Gloria—whose very name is an ironic play upon that of her real-life original—a prototype for one phase of America: corrupted in its youth, it grows (but does not grow up) into a wild, dissolute beauty. Too, O'Hara creates her as another of his rebels, one not consciously in revolt and not specifically against any abstraction of "society," but one rebelling against the sort of hypocritical respectability O'Hara himself despised.

Essentially, *Butterfield* 8 can be interpreted as another version of the situation in *Appointment in Samarra*: a beautiful or potentially beautiful young person commits suicide because of self-disgust stemming originally from a failure of love. Although

Gloria's life does not end with a deliberate act of suicide, her demise proceeds directly from a life lived suicidally. Her drinking, reliance on drugs, promiscuity, and total lack of purpose are all self-destructive; even had she not died accidentally her behavior would in time produce her death as surely as Julian's planned act ended his existence.

Gloria's parents cannot be blamed so directly for her inner torment as Dr. English can for Julian's, but nevertheless they and others have failed her. They indulge her when they should have controlled and chastened, while the two most important men in her life, Eddie Brunner and Weston Liggett, both fall short of the overreaching act of love which might have made all the difference. However, Eddie is not strong enough to overcome his scruples about Gloria's promiscuity, and Liggett is driven by his own selfish passion. In a sense each man behaves according to the dictates of his own nature and thus evades the full guilt for Gloria's death. But their consistency comes at the expense of the woman they both love; and, if the conditions of existence are such that they cannot be blamed for acting as they must, still the bitter irony is that they do not act well enough to save a life.

Like Julian, too, Gloria approaches the moment of self-discovery just before she dies. Although the narrative spans only a few days and Gloria has been engaged in debauchery for some five years, something has happened to her—we are not sure what—which will soon change this situation. When she awakens in Liggett's apartment sick with shame and self-disgust, as she has awakened so many times before in other places, she feels she is at last on the verge of realizing what drives her to act as she does. She has too little time left to find out, but later developments in the narrative indicate that her growth into maturity as a person and as a woman has finally commenced. She will begin to conclude that she wants motherhood, that marriage and marital fidelity are more than shibboleths, and that deep sexual experience with one man is infintely preferable to sex with a thousand, no matter how wild or skillful lovers they may be.

As for Gloria's beauty, it is not of face and body alone, and certainly not yet of soul, but a trait of personality. She has that animal magnetism, that quality, like Julian English, of lending zest and excitement to a place and people by her

very presence. Strangely enough, she also conveys a kind of innocence or wonder at life (a characteristic among those suggested by her name), as though her growth had been arrested
at the age when the older man had molested her. And, finally,
in Gloria is transmitted the power of sex and something of
its essence, of sex unhampered by restraint and protocol, and
often, in fact, in defiance of them. She has had affairs by the
dozen, but ultimately only three men have meaning to her
sexually: the first man to know her, from whom she learns
that sex can enslave; the man she doesn't have, Eddie Brunner;
and the man who shows her more nakedly than anyone else the
intensity of his desire, Weston Liggett. There are moments of
tenderness—especially in the scene with Eddie, the near-con-
summation which could have changed her life—but the truth
about sex reveals itself most directly in what it does to Liggett, who despite previous affairs has always preserved his
home, marriage, and independence until his desire for Gloria
overwhelms him and makes him risk all. In her own way Gloria
is Aphrodite, Astarte, against whom no man is proof.

Other than its trenchant portrayal of the sexual force, the
most remarkable aspect of *Butterfield 8* is its value and function
as a document of a moment in social history: the Speakeasy
period and the people who typified it. Throughout the novel,
indeed as its main setting, there is the Speakeasy, which O'Hara
describes in all its kinds and varieties with the vividness and
expert knowledge of the historian-reporter, the chronicler of
the age he was later to announce himself to be. Not only does
the depiction convince us of its authenticity, it is also funny,
sad, alluring, repulsive, exhilarating, and depressing—all these
at once. Socially, the Speakeasy represents a type of democracy;
it is one of the few places where the rich and famous, powerful
and titled mix on equal terms with the low, humble, average,
obscure. Further, for its patrons it serves as a harlequin mask,
covering depravity with a frenzied grin. It is where one goes to
wash away in a flood of alcohol and laughter the latest sadness
and sin.

O'Hara takes his readers inside a number of such places
and tells what they are like; more important, he captures
the feel of Speakeasy life. There are society matrons who have
come to New York from other cities to view obscene movies and
to sleep with a lover. There are Hollywood people, each with

his secret crimes carefully hidden from an adoring public's glance. There are eminent ladies whose husbands have infected them with venereal disease, and there are debutantes who act as dope suppliers for high society. There are foreign diplomats whose morals fall far short of their prestigious positions. There are artists, showgirls, procurers. There are men with friendly manner who are, in fact, consumed by their inner anger and frustration. There are jockeys, and owners of Rolls Royces, and film actresses.[6] All of it is a glittering, depraved circus; and Gloria in her own way is its embodiment.

The novel sets forth other bits of information about New York which vividly re-create the city in the first years of the Depression: the scarcity of jobs, the possibility of dying an obscure death, the vicious power of gangsters (one of them hosts a party during which, "for laughs," a naked girl is hung out of a window thirty-five stories up, held only by knotted bedsheets tied around her ankle), the struggles of unknown young men from the provinces hoping to cash in on their talent, the violence everywhere just underneath the surface, ready to break out. Altogether, O'Hara succeeds in capturing the time's instability and hysteria. Occasionally one hears the prediction that in the next few years there will be revolution; and, while such uppercrust characters as Liggett scoff at any such eventuality, the novel persuades that neither revolution nor the apocalypse is beyond the realm of possibility.

Unhappily the book's workmanship exhibits a number of grave defects which offset much of its achievement. Although O'Hara employs techniques similar to those in *Appointment in Samarra*—the shifting perspective and the alternation of action and stasis—in *Butterfield 8* these devices fall short of the consistency and effectiveness of the earlier work. Furthermore, in this, O'Hara's second novel, one already observes defects that later damage some of his Pennsylvania sagas: preoccupation with case history and social backgrounds, characters whose presence in the tale cannot be fully justified on esthetic grounds, and tenuous motivation for the behavior of major characters. Of these characters, Gloria is especially baffling. Just when the reader thinks he understands her, she suddenly behaves unpredictably—especially in her relationship with Liggett. She over-reacts to all he says and does, up to the moment of her death. Her death, too, although O'Hara foreshadows it carefully from the novel's very start, still seems gratuitous in its circumstances. Perhaps in O'Hara's defense one might argue that he wished his portrayal to be accurate to its documentary source, that Starr Faithfull herself lived and died gratuitously, unpredictably. There is even a curious consistency between the real world which inspired O'Hara's rendition and the novel in which he captures it; for one can say of both that, with all their flaws, they retain for us a certain raw power and memorableness.

II *The Author as Protagonist in* Hope of Heaven *and Other Fiction*

On its own merits O'Hara's third novel, *Hope of Heaven* (1938), supplies no basis for prolonged consideration; it is a slight and ephemeral piece. Essentially a love story about the romance between Jim Malloy and Peggy Henderson, the novel once more illustrates that tendency toward fatalism especially evident in O'Hara's poorer work; for the lovers are separated by circumstance at the crucial point in their relationship. Things happen, sometimes for the better, sometimes for the worse; or so reads the book's most profound implicit conclusion. As social history the novel has a somewhat greater claim upon one's attention in its treatment of a phase of national culture, Hollywood. Although the reader learns little about the film industry *per se*, O'Hara does transmit the feel, the mood of Hollywood life as experienced by one of its lower echelons, the second-string film writers.

However, from another standpoint *Hope of Heaven* has special interest to the student of O'Hara's career because it is the only book in which the writer assumes the role of his own protagonist in the person of Jim Malloy. Together with *Butterfield 8* and a number of shorter fictions, it comprises a minor saga or chronicle, the Malloy-O'Hara saga. I shall trace this motif as it occurs in the pages of O'Hara's New York-Hollywood fiction.

Older now than the Malloy who appeared briefly in *Butterfield 8*, and divorced, Malloy continues to be the passionate romantic beneath his callous and worldly exterior. He likes the affluent style of his life as a screen writer, but he views his work largely as a means to an end. Despite his materialism he remains acutely sympathetic. He has no specific political affiliation, yet he feels strongly enough to declare: "I haven't got a good thinking brain, but I have sound emotions. . . . I know almost right away, without thinking, without using words like activize and ideology and dialectic materialism and all that crap, I am on the right side. That is, the leftist side."[7] Finally, one perceives of Malloy that, with all his friends and activities, he is fundamentally solitary.

This self-projection continues in other instances of O'Hara's work, revealing further truths about the writer-protagonist and with considerably more artistic success than that achieved in *Hope of Heaven*. *Hellbox* (1947), a collection of short stories, includes a cluster of autobiographical pieces having Malloy as their protagonist or narrator. Three of these stories are roughly sequential. In the first of them, "Transaction," Malloy purchases a Duesenberg sedan from a genteelly poor Harvard law student and his wife, a car Malloy drives on his leisurely way west to Hollywood. In the second story, he encounters en route an old sweetheart, now resident instructor in a women's junior college, when he aids one of the school's students marooned with her escort after an automobile accident. In the third, "Pardner," he describes his meeting with a seemingly tough, cocky young restaurant proprietor who is actually as comically gullible as a child. Of the three, "Transaction" is simultaneously the most illuminating and the best-executed. What seems to be a routine episode, routinely narrated, is actually a subtle, multi-layered construction.

The Duesenberg sedan which Malloy purchases is not only a superb machine, it also signifies power, elegance, quality. Its acquisition is thus fraught with significance. One should note the implications communicated in this dialogue between Malloy and Mrs. Van Buren (the name evidences the lady's breeding, as contrasted to her present circumstances):

> "You're a writer, aren't you? I'm ashamed to confess I've never read anything you've written."
>
> "The world is full of people that haven't read anything I've written. I'm a screen writer, Mrs. Van Buren."
>
> "Oh, well that must be interesting too."
>
> "It buys Duesenbergs," he said. "I'd rather be right here."
>
> "Why? You didn't by any chance go to Harvard, did you?"
>
> "No, I most certainly did not, or anywhere else. That's probably why I'd rather be here."
>
> She laughed. "That *might* explain it."[8]

Further, the story concludes with an episode not so simple as it seems: Malloy's gesture in paying an additional seventy-five dollars for an accessory the Van Burens would include without charge. First, Malloy's act conveys his tribute to this struggling but closely knit young couple willing to forego present pleasures for deeper future satisfactions. Second, Malloy's manner of presenting the money reflects the delicacy of his own social instincts: he realizes the Van Burens would not accept a gift and are too naïve to demand the highest price for the accessory that the buyer would pay. By insisting that *he* be allowed to decide the object's value, Malloy can give them money they need while sparing them the embarrassment of asking for it. Third, the last detail of this transaction connotes Malloy's ambivalent self-regard. The extra seventy-five dollar payment serves to assuage his submerged guilt that, as a *nouveau-riche* Hollywood writer, he has the means to acquire an object belonging to someone more deserving; but, at the same time, he takes comfort from his ability to spend the sum without a moment's hesitation. And at this point, once the story's dimensions have been estimated, its autobiographical interest becomes subordinate to its artistic function.

Malloy also figures in some of O'Hara's recent work, most notably in the three praiseworthy *novellas* comprising *Sermons and Soda Water* (1960), which bring the Malloy-O'Hara saga through the 1930's and even into a few moments of the present. The parts of *Sermons and Soda Water* have the tone of memoirs, and as such they have a confessional function. Most important they corroborate one crucial fact about their author-protagonist already suggested in *Butterfield 8* and *Hope of Heaven:* the fact of a profound, abiding, and pervasive loneliness. The whirl of day and night activity, the multitude of beautiful and sexy women who parade through Malloy's life, the concern with the experience of others, the crowded recollections of his youth: all are but sops to what seems the dominant emotional truth about Malloy-O'Hara—loneliness.

Nor is loneliness exclusively the narrator's affliction. Charlotte Sears, the glamorous movie star, is lonely (*The Girl on the Baggage Truck*). Bobbie and Pete McCrea of Gibbsville are lonely during most of the years of their troubled marriage (*Imagine Kissing Pete*). Charley Ellis faces the unbearable loneliness of life without his wife Nancy, when she dies suddenly (*We're Friends Again*). In a sense, loneliness and what people do to combat it constitute the major theme of these *novellas,* as it also constitutes one of the central concerns of O'Hara's fiction. Among the loneliest of O'Hara characters is Jim Malloy, who says of himself just after the end of a love affair: "I was being resentenced to the old frenetic loneliness that none of us would admit to, but that governed our habits and our lives." And the last of the *novellas* concludes in this fashion, a conclusion applicable to more than this particular tale:

> I knew this man so well, and with his permission, but I had never heard him make such an outright declaration of love for his wife, and on my way home I realized that until then I had not known him at all. It was not a discovery to cause me dismay. What did he know about me? What, really, can any of us know about any of us, and why must we make such a thing of loneliness when it is the final condition of us all? And where would love be without it?[9]

Viewed in the large, then, O'Hara's self-projection as Malloy serves two functions in his career. The first and most obvious of these, the autobiographical, has been stressed. From Malloy-O'Hara one adduces information interesting for its own sake and useful in the interpretation of the writer's work. For example, Malloy displays in all his fictive appearances the same enormous sensitivity to people—their dress, clothes, speech, manners and their intelligence and moral fiber as well—as does John O'Hara the writer in the practice of his craft. The mixture of toughness and tenderness, solitariness and gregariousness, pride and humility that are characteristic of Malloy undoubtedly also pertains to O'Hara himself. Above all, in the portrayal of Malloy one observes O'Hara's candor, including an element of explicit self-hatred, a candor which enables the reader to conclude of Malloy that he is neither wholly likeable nor admirable. The conclusion is in itself a testimony to the writer's honesty.

Second, Malloy performs an artistic task: he provides a link between the disparate components of O'Hara's New York-Hollywood writing. Shortcomings accruing to this entire body of work prevent Malloy from serving in this function as valuably as he might; but in himself, judged as fictional character and protagonist, he nonetheless bids inclusion among O'Hara's more vivid and memorable creations.

III   Pal Joey: *The Triumph of Vernacular*

The grave deficiencies of *Hope of Heaven* must be set against
O'Hara's triumph in his story-sequence published two years later,
Pal Joey (1940).[10] With their malapropisms, erratic spelling,
grammatical blunders and mangled punctuation, together with
the exhibition of their fictional writer's roguery, these "letters"
from the irrepressible Joey to his friend Ted demand consideration as one of those minor comic masterpieces of American literature which have survived because of their surprising vitality and
stamina. As one reads these missives, recorded monologues really,
one is reminded of native Western humor of the sort first embodied in the performances of Artemus Ward and Josh Billings,
reaching its apogee in Twain, and continuing its thrust
into the present century: the straight-faced drollery with its
undertone of irony and its implicit amazement at the varieties
of human folly. As practiced by its nineteenth-century originators,
such humor derived much of its effect from a distancing technique. In this technique the speaker or observer took the attitude
of the countryman, the commonsensical practical man of the soil,
looking out at the incredible antics of the supposedly more
civilized and educated residents of the big city. The larger and
more famous the city, the more asinine is the behavior of its
citizens—and the more sardonically droll the observations of the
commentator.

One of the fundamental characteristics of this tradition of
American humor is the use of the vernacular, of an unmistakably
American voice speaking in an obviously native idiom. Thus,
while its practitioners in the last few generations have been
such dissimilar performers as Irvin S. Cobb and Will Rogers,
Ring Lardner and Damon Runyon, some continuing the tradition
in oral delivery and others in writing, their indebtedness to
the basic techniques and attitudes of Western humor is irrefragable. Each practitioner has adapted the tradition according
to his own methods, purposes, and idiom: sometimes speaking
as rustic philosopher, sometimes as baseball player, sometimes
as denizen of Broadway bars. A number of the most distinguished
fiction writers of this century have also practiced in this tradition: Sinclair Lewis in his satirical monologues, Sherwood Anderson, Hemingway, Faulkner, Wolfe. It is also perhaps what

Salinger does best. The awareness of the tradition lurks behind Hemingway's remark that all American literature began with a book by Mark Twain, for Hemingway had reference primarily to Huck's native speaking voice and to those inflections and locutions, simple, direct, seemingly artless, in which the voice told what the world was like. And the mixture of ignorance and knowledge, innocence and experience, idealism and cynicism, joy and sadness conveyed in the tone of that voice was as basic to its authenticity, its Americanness, as the words in which it spoke.

So in *Pal Joey* O'Hara has captured the true accents of a second-rate night club entertainer, and along with him permanently recorded a minor but yet typical and fascinating segment of American life. Perhaps the most remarkable aspect of these stories, although one does not realize it immediately, is their Americanness. They could have been written in no other country. Joey is a rogue-hero: brash, egotistical, vulgar, forever on the make for a pretty girl or a fast buck; he has elastic morals and not much capacity (or opportunity) for loyalty, friendship, truth; but he is also somehow winning in his insouciance, drive, hunger for life. To take Joey at his own word, he is tough, cocky, smart, never at a loss for a quick reply or a shrewd maneuver; yet a closer inspection shows him to be essentially innocent, sentimental, ineffectual, a sucker for a hard-luck story ("Joey and the Calcutta Club") and often prey for the bigger animals in the jungle he inhabits ("Joey on Herta"). Proud of his success with women, his wiles fool only naïve young college girls, those fresh from the farm, mentally dull chorines, or unsophisticated stenographers. Whenever he encounters an experienced or intelligent woman, as in "Joey and Mavis" or in "A Bit of a Shock," he is at their mercy. Either they dupe him or else use his sexual capacity, which is considerable, for their own satisfaction.

What makes Joey more appealing than the other show-business types who troupe through O'Hara's fiction during the 1930's and early 1940's in such large numbers is that beneath his braggadocio, one discerns the shape of a human being. Not of sterling substance to begin with and further hardened and cheapened by his way of life, he remains in part a boy, with a boy's capacity for enthusiasm, a boy's excitement about new people and places, and a boy's yearning for the insignia of success. There is also something of the Babbitt in him. Although he pretends to sneer at those rooted in established jobs, homes, and marriages, we sense a longing for the regularity, security, and comfort Joey affects to despise. What he really wanted was to marry the banker's daughter who had become infatuated with him, settle down with her, take a job in her father's business, join the country club, and live happily in Ohio forever after. But bad luck (he is extraordinarily unlucky), his own large vanity, and his incapacity to coldheadedly carry his plan through foiled his chances at the moment of their culmination ("Ex-Pal" and "How I Am New in Chi").

One other important distinction that must be made between Joey and O'Hara's other, less attractive Broadway and Hollywood characters, is that while they are childish, Joey is childlike. Their *metier*, with its emphasis upon personal aggrandizement, hardly encourages emotional maturity, nor is Joey very much more mature than his brethren. But much of Joey's behavior depends upon a simple naïveté as to the nature of human nature, and his defeats more often than not stem from this innocence. As shrewd as he is in petty matters—getting a few extra dollars in salary, improving his billing, devising a strategem to attract a pretty girl—he continues to be innocent enough to take people at their appearance, to judge them as they wish to be judged. Consequently, because he fails to penetrate surfaces, he is continually being surprised when another sheds his disguise and deliberately reveals his actual identity to Joey, as in "The Erloff." He is especially vulnerable before anyone wearing the guise of respectability.

In contrast, the Broadway and Hollywood folk in dozens of O'Hara's other stories are autistic rather than innocent. Although the needs and feelings of others are simply of no consequence to them, they develop a keen ability to perceive the bases of others' behavior and to turn that knowledge to their own account. Crossed, they sulk, throw tantrums, seek revenge, and are placated only when their own wills have prevailed. Incapable of any consistency of emotion or concentration, they acquire new baubles, new people, new distractions; they are like children who turn from one interest to the next when each loses its allure, as it always quickly does. None of these tendencies are true of Joey. Perhaps he would be spoiled and toughened by success, thereby losing his capacity to view his defeats with wry humor, one of his most attractive traits. But, as O'Hara presents him, Joey is among the most appealing of the numerous breed populating the New York-Hollywood fiction.

Moreover, this intriguing and amusing character comes to life in a series of monologues which show O'Hara at his best. While there is no real symmetry or structure either to the entire sequence or in its individual episodes, each tale moves so swiftly and is so packed with anecdote that the lack of controlled form elsewhere damaging to O'Hara's fiction seems unimportant here. The people Joey meets, the experiences he has, and above all his own thoughts and responses are rendered with such exuberance and deftness that one is content simply to read on. There are no abstractions; everything is concrete and particular: names, places, actions, songs, clothes, cars, what Joey said and what the others said—all is rendered in Joey's distinctive voice. The total impression created by O'Hara is therefore that of the absolute, vivid reality attained when a writer achieves the triumph of completely vanishing into his material and his invented character.

IV *Broadway and Hollywood in the Short Stories*

The collections of short stories which O'Hara published during the 1930's and 1940's reflect his preoccupation with the entertainment world to which he was himself affiliated. The stirrings of this interest are apparent in the first of these volumes, *The Doctor's Son and Other Stories* (1935), which contains six tales of the Broadway-Hollywood genre, one of them ("Master of Ceremonies") prefiguring the *Pal Joey* sketches. Interest becomes obsession in *Files on Parade* (1939), for almost half the pieces in this collection are concerned with show business. That the writer's attention was turning to other matters is obvious in two later volumes, *Pipe Night* (1945) and *Hellbox* (1947), the latter containing only four tales utilizing Broadway-Hollywood characters and situations.

Files on Parade illustrates both the vices and virtues of O'Hara's show-business fiction. While some of these stories are effectively satirical studies of various stage and screen types, the nature of their subject matter obstructs profundity or real seriousness even when O'Hara writes the sort of quietly savage exposé of the utter heartlessness and egotism of some film queen, as in "Sidesaddle" and "Most Gorgeous Thing"—the kind of story he does best in this genre.

Although O'Hara plumbs such characters to their vulgar depths, their depths lie just beneath the surface. Once the writer has slashed through the dazzling veneer of these celebrities, once he has attuned the reader to the special frequency of their talk, once he has taken us backstage or on the set, once he has exposed their venality and ruthlessness, we have learned all. As illustrated by *Pal Joey*, O'Hara can portray his Broadway-Hollywood "small fry" with affection and humor despite their frailties. But as if by some barometric response to their power and fame, the closer O'Hara's characters are to the top of their world, the harsher his treatment is likely to be.

Of all these types, that which most fascinates O'Hara and which he depicts most vividly is the successful stage or film actress, a type one may infer from his stories (many of them cast in the first-person narrator mode) that O'Hara has studied through close personal contact. Certainly, his own experience as press agent and movie writer provided ample opportunity for direct observation. O'Hara's treatment of these women nearly always conveys some ambivalence, for they are presented with a mixture of loathing, admiration, hatred, and desire. They are the deadliest predators in the show business jungle, at least to a male; for, despite the soiled condition of their souls, they are also beautiful—irresistibly so—feminine, charming, and consummately skilled in the arts of love. Whatever one may feel about them as human beings, whatever moral outrage a man must commit to gain their favor, his own sexual desires give them the mastery over him because they are aware of their effect upon him and they know exactly how to exploit it. While they themselves are capable of enjoying sexual pleasure—indeed they may *need* it also—their erotic appetites are always subordinated to other, more material ends. Unlike the males whom they bend to their wills, they do not romanticize and idealize sex; they use it but do not deify it. Thus they become its masters.

Although glamorous film stars serve as the subject for many stories throughout O'Hara's career, his treatment is illustrated perfectly in *Files on Parade* in the story "Sidesaddle," wherein a movie queen of the sort just described wheedles her ex-husband into giving her a saddle having to him something of the status and importance of a family heirloom. His reward? A little romp in the hay before her current husband returns from a trip. Why does he do it? Because he can't help it. When she asks him early in the story for a favor as yet unspecified, his response is, inevitably: "All right. What is it you want? You know you'll get it, especially the way you look now. God damn it."[11] Why does she do it? Regardless of her avowed reasons, plausible on their surface, one suspects that her actual motivations are, first, to discover whether she still has power over her ex-husband; second, to strike back at his family whom the reader infers did not admire her; third, to wound her ex-husband's sister who uses and treasures the saddle; and, fourth, to secure an object possessing a certain social "class" which will be especially prestigious in traditionless Hollywood.

As this summation implies, "Sidesaddle" is an impressively subtle story conveying a number of nuances and dimensions of meaning and characterization, but what lingers in the memory is the image of corruption. Behind the ex-husband's behavior one almost hears the echoes of ringing bells and slobbering dogs. Unhappily for O'Hara's ultimate achievement as an artist, however, this story and others equally able and equally disturbing often lack the symbolic quality which would enable the reader to generalize, and so interpret the Broadway-Hollywood people as metaphors of the human condition. As is, these characters as well as the stories which contain them remain only extremely vivid vignettes of a special, limited world.

Occasionally O'Hara presents his Broadway-Hollywood types with winning compassion. Thus in "Common Sense Should Tell You" (*Hellbox*) he portrays with much less than ordinary malice one of his enormously powerful, self-indulgent film executives. The man has just been informed by his doctors that all further indulgence threatens his life, and yet he is so enamoured of his pleasures and so conditioned to give his senses full play that he cannot restrain his instincts and desires. In the same collection "Drawing Room B" offers a perceptive and at last affirmative depiction of an aging movie actress returning from a week in New York, during which she has been tormented by loneliness and the evidence of her decline. "Call Me, Call Me," published in the recent collection *Assembly*, likewise sympathetically treats an over-age, now virtually forgotten actress, while the depiction of Charlotte Sears in *Sermons and Soda Water* constitutes one of the most attractive portraits of women in O'Hara's entire body of work.

O'Hara has also recently used his Broadway-Hollywood material to greater than usual advantage by juxtaposing entertainers and their peculiar outlook with the lives and attitudes of other kinds of people. In Part I of *Sermons and Soda Water* he skillfully blends and contrasts stage and film celebrities with the New York and Long Island rich; and in "The Girl from California" (*Assembly*) he presents a situation wherein a young movie star and his bride, herself a star, visit the groom's lower middle-class family in the East. Herein O'Hara convincingly evokes the tensions and the unresolved family problems which confront the successful son upon his return home. Not only does O'Hara catch the ambiguous status and emotions of the visiting son, deeply attached to his family but already isolated from it by his new fame and riches; he also suggests the inescapable conflict in the situation. Despite the protagonist's good intentions, the visit swiftly and predictably turns sour. His wife, having already been tempered by the same ordeal with her own people, declares the sad conclusion: "They hate us, they all hate us. Either way, they hate us. If we're nice, they hate us just as much as if we treat them like dirt ... Erase them from your mind, honey. It's the best way."[12]

Such fine pieces as these are the exception rather than the rule. Too often O'Hara repeats himself in his Broadway-Hollywood tales. Again and again he presents the beautiful, sexy actress with the morals of a mink, using her sexuality as a commodity to be bartered for services rendered ("Can You Carry Me?" and "Fire" in *Pipe Night*), or the Hollywood bigwig who would be contemptible if he were not so powerful ("Mr. Sidney Gainsborough: Quality Pictures" in *The Doctor's Son and Other Stories*). O'Hara's gains as a satirist in these and other tales do not deter cognizance that he is merely exercising an already proven facility. Furthermore, the Broadway-Hollywood stories somehow seem to elicit the worst in the writer. "Adventure on the Set" (*Pipe Night*), for example, is a trivial re-run of the *Pal Joey* mode but with a less appealing protagonist; and "Reunion Over Lightly" (*Pipe Night*) is an infuriatingly obscure piece packed with pointless innuendo.

The student of O'Hara's career therefore requires little reflection to formulate an equation which can be applied, with a few exceptions, to O'Hara's several volumes of short stories: since the weakest volume, *Files on Parade,* is precisely that with the largest number of Broadway-Hollywood tales, and since the weakest portions of the other collections of the 1930's and 1940's are likewise Broadway-Hollywood stories, and since the generally admirable later collections (*Assembly* and others) contain the fewest such stories, *ergo:* John O'Hara succeeds as a serious and enduring writer of short stories exactly in proportion to the distance he maintains between himself and Broadway-Hollywood.

V Five Plays: *New York and Hollywood as Drama*

Considering his equipment and his methods, one might expect O'Hara to be an outstanding dramatist. His ability to create an intensely visualized scene, his understanding of the tensions and conflicts roiling under seemingly limpid surfaces, his superb control of dialogue, his sense of what might be called in dramaturgical terms "timing" (especially as he demonstrates it in the short story), his concern with psychological interaction, the economy and directness of language which obtains in his best work: all these promise that O'Hara might have become a distinguished playwright had he so chosen. Play-writing would also seem a logical extension of O'Hara's work for the films. Unfortunately, there is ample evidence that he did so choose, at least during one recent interval in his career, but with little success.

In *Five Plays* (1961), O'Hara presents virtually all his writing for the theater, omitting only the libretto of *Pal Joey.* As the volume's foreword states, the plays were completed between 1952 and 1961 and written because it pleased O'Hara to do so. The foreword also briefly sets forth something of the circumstances of composition of each play, and closes with O'Hara's embarrassingly defensive assault on "creative" directors, an assault whose thesis is announced in its opening sentence: "Some, or maybe all, of these plays would have reached Broadway if I had been willing to take writing lessons from directors, but I know of no director whose writing talent I respect. Nor do I know of any director whose contribution to a production will guarantee a hit. Since he cannot guarantee a hit, why not do it your way and succeed or fail on your own?"[13] Whatever the validity of O'Hara's comments, they do not explain the infirmities of his own work.

One of O'Hara's great strengths as a fiction writer is his ability to depict the sudden, startling, but convincing expression of evil that he sees as inherent in the makeup of many men and women, an evil often manifested in some vicious, callous, or selfish act. Yet aside from Joe Rogg, the surly truck-driver in *The Farmer's Hotel,* none of the scores of characters in these plays really displays any capacity for evil. Acts, thoughts, words which O'Hara would have treated as *evil* in a story or novel become merely nasty, unpleasant, or weak. This fuzziness of treatment becomes especially detrimental to the total effect of the plays when one recalls that four of the five involve violent death caused by murder or suicide. This frequency of death and violence, and the playwright's use of it to culminate a drama, would ordinarily suggest to the audience the writer's mordant vision, his tragic view of life; but O'Hara's plays unfortunately contain no substantiation for such a conclusion. Except in *The Farmer's Hotel* one can discern no vision of any kind.

In other words, O'Hara has employed some of the machinery and attributes of tragedy, or at least of serious drama, without a corresponding emotional or philosophical context. The result is melodrama, entertainment, diversion. At best, these plays seem about equal in quality to the run-of-the-mill offering of most Broadway seasons, but mediocrity is not the usual standard of comparison appropriate for John O'Hara.

For example, *The Searching Sun* ends with two shocking suicides: first, Zita kills herself upon realizing that her stepfather (whom she loves and with whom she has just had an affair) would sacrifice her in order to advance his stage career; a few moments later she is followed by Archie, the stepfather-lover, presumably because of the shame and self-disgust aroused by Zita's death. Yet the characters have not earlier displayed those traits which would render their self-annihilation dramatically convincing. Zita could not possibly have felt any shock upon learning of her stepfather's duplicity because she had long known him to be a spineless cad. She had seen him love and abandon a succession of just such girls as herself. Furthermore, Zita is portrayed throughout the play as a remarkably healthy and stable young woman, the kind of girl her own mother depicts as spending "half her life in boats, the other half on skis." Whatever hurts she suffers do not add up to suicide. A good cry, perhaps, or even a break with her family, but no more. And Archie, a suicide? Archie is a man who in the play's first scene makes a fuss over a burned finger. Having come to know such characters as Zita and Archie for an entire play, how can one accept their dazzling reversal of form in the drama's closing moments?

Unconvincing characterization also plagues *Veronique*, which is a persistently unattractive piece of work. Veronique herself, the play's central figure, alternates throughout between great stupidity and great wisdom, innocence and worldliness, impulsiveness and restraint, complaisance and stubbornness. Perhaps there are such people; perhaps there was one whom O'Hara knew in his Greenwich Village days and used as the model for this character. If so, it was the writer's duty to bring her to life in his play and not merely to transport her from life into his work. Other elements in the play are equally unreal. There is, for example, a concluding scene in which Veronique, suddenly cleansed of hatred, forgives the man who has murdered her sister. The murderer himself, once a hysterical homosexual, has meanwhile found God. I find it appalling that O'Hara the tough-minded Realist, the slashing satirist and parodist, the "Impersonal Ironist of the Single Vision" as a hostile but impressed reviewer once called him, should write such patently absurd and melodramatic scenes.

Happily, the other plays in the volume are somewhat better, or at least more tightly written. Little need be said about *The Farmer's Hotel*, since it is almost identical to the dramatic portions of the *novella*. It remains a commendable piece of work. Although *The Way It Was* defies judgment in its present form, that of a scenario or libretto, and although it, too, suffers from thinness of substance and from insufficiently developed motivation, one can visualize it in production. With the right music and staging, it could possibly be even more successful than the adaptation of *Pal Joey*, which was first produced in 1940 and then revived in 1952, on the latter occasion winning awards as the best musical of the season.[14] Indeed, even in outline *The Way It Was* seems both more poignant and less contrived than the *Pal Joey* libretto. One wonders why some farsighted theatrical entrepreneur has not already produced it.

The Champagne Pool is, except for *The Farmer's Hotel*,

the most carefully constructed and credibly motivated of the five plays, but its subject matter suffers from triviality. Once more O'Hara returns to the Broadway theater world and its people for his situation and characters: the conniving but irresistible actress, the venal producer, the crass, irritating but sensitive and honest director, and so on. There is little that has not been presented before.

However, *The Champagne Pool* does contain passages which illuminate the urgent question of why so gifted a writer as O'Hara should issue such inferior work as is contained in *Five Plays*. In a number of dialogues between Frank Wilson, a successful novelist who has turned to drama, and Joe Rasmussen, a director who has heretofore specialized in hard-boiled Realism, one perceives that O'Hara's failure as a dramatist lies not in the carelessness of his work but in the mistaken direction of his ambitions. The fictive Wilson and Rasmussen, who together comprise the real O'Hara, both aspire to write light comedy and sophisticated satire in the manner of Philip Barry and S. N. Behrman. Thus, *The Champagne Pool* is not only a play about the attempt to restore such work as Philip Barry's to the modern theater, it is a play by an author who is himself attempting to emulate Philip Barry. The felony is compounded, moreover, in that four of O'Hara's five compositions for the stage deal with show business or are somehow involved with its people —topics in themselves lacking urgency.

O'Hara has written his plays as though there had been no Ibsen, Chekhov, O'Neill, Arthur Miller, Tennessee Williams. These plays have a curiously old-fashioned, even "well-made" quality. They remind one of the sort of transition drama being done around the turn of the century by what might be called the drawing-room Realists, Pinero and Jones, for example, or the earliest Shaw. Although O'Hara employs such superficies of Realism as violence, profanity, and illicit sexuality, such matters as society, life, and art are not submitted to close examination in these plays. One gets nowhere in this volume the sense of crisis, the apocalyptic vision, the moral agony, the assault upon sanity, the excruciating inquiry into the basic conditions of human existence, the protest against social injustice, the divining after the wellsprings of thought and feeling, which one finds everywhere in the work of the famous dramatists who make modern drama the vital and exciting genre it is. In brief, the larger basis for rejection of O'Hara as a playwright is that he cannot be taken seriously.

VI   The Big Laugh: *The Problem of Character Change*

Tucked in among the Pennsylvania sagas and the volumes of expertly crafted short fiction characteristic of O'Hara's career since 1949 is a second Hollywood novel, *The Big Laugh* (1961). It, together with the collection of plays, and a sprinkling of recent stories, signifies the writer's continuing enchantment with his Broadway-Hollywood experience. It also reaffirms his intimate knowledge of that world, its moving forces, its atmosphere, and the behavior patterns of its folk. One might even surmise that such characters as Hubert Ward, Joe Ziffrin, Martin Ruskin, Charley Simmons, Jack Golson, and Doris Arlington have in whole or in part true-life originals. Certainly they represent authentic show business types.[15] Furthermore, O'Hara sketches quite graphically the power struggles, the economic pressures, the caste system, and the social activity which distinguish life in Hollywood from life everywhere else. He also captures and sympathetically conveys the special loneliness and peculiar emotional privation which the film star must endure.

The Big Laugh, then, is not hampered by dubious authenticity. Nor is it devoid of good writing. The entire episode involving the triangle of Charley and Mildred Simmons and Hubie Ward (faintly reminiscent of Fitzgerald's "Crazy Sunday" and perhaps based upon the same real-life source) is exceedingly well done, especially O'Hara's portrayal of Charley Simmons as a man who has gained the world and lost his soul. There are also superbly funny and plausible monologues by two classic Hollywood types, the semiliterate, crude, but amazingly cunning producer, and the even more vulgar but equally perceptive agent.

Observe the mind of Hiram J. Zimmerman (Hollywood producer) in action as he visualizes the proper role for his new find, Hubert Ward:

"Hubert Ward is a young fellow comes to this typical American town. He meets say Mary Brian. Pretty, innocent, good respectable family and maybe George Bancroft for her father. Or maybe we put it down South and let Miriam Hopkins play the daughter. Anyway, Hubert comes to town and starts monkeying around with Mary Brian. She gets knocked up and Hubert deserts her in her condition. How we're ever gonna get this by the Hays Office I don't know, but we can skirt around as much as we can. What I want is to see this young fellow get his just deserts. I want to see George Bancroft give him a good beating. Kick the living shit out of the son of a bitch. Maybe Mary's really in love with Phil Holmes, her childhood sweetheart. I don't know. I just thought of this idea during lunch, but I'm convinced. If we can make the American audience hate this young fellow enough, he could turn into an American Stroheim. A clean-cut heavy. That would be revolutionary, and the foreign market would eat it up. They're always complaining about our stories, we'll give them something sophisticated, and at the same time hold on to our American audience."[16]

This writing, in its authenticity of idiom and bawdy humor, challenges the best work of such American masters of the monologue as Sinclair Lewis and Ring Lardner. However, despite the humor and gusto attained in segments of *The Big Laugh*, it is plagued by two of O'Hara's most lamentable failings: (1) weakness of structure, and (2) unconvincingly motivated characters.

As in other flawed O'Hara novels, *The Big Laugh* begins well, builds to a crisis too early, and then trails off. Nothing else in the story achieves the intensity and power of the episode ending in Charley Simmons' death, an episode occurring almost exactly halfway through the novel. The romance between Hubie and Nina and the account of Hubie's rise to stardom both hold the attention, but there is nothing to climax them. Both are predictable. O'Hara attempts to provide a high point of interest late in the book by re-introducing Hubie's first antagonist, Martin Ruskin; but the whole action concerned with Ruskin smacks of contrivance. Although the novel closes with a brilliantly executed kaleidoscope of Hubie's recent past and probable future, this display of O'Hara's skill does not redeem what has already been forfeited.

The structural blemishes of *The Big Laugh* are emphasized by an even more tangible deficiency in characterization. The characters are treated imperfectly in two ways: first, their motivations are not made fully clear or convincing; second, the reader cannot completely involve himself with them or even take any sort of firm stance toward them because O'Hara himself is ambivalent.

The central problem in O'Hara's handling of character is

that of change. Again and again in O'Hara, including the opening pages of *The Big Laugh,* one finds the declaration that all change in the personality and character of human beings comes slowly, if at all; and, even when change is possible, few are capable of very much of it in a lifetime. Indeed, one of O'Hara's great strengths and one of his most persuasive and terrifying effects is the portrayal of a man's destiny flowing slowly out of the condition of his character as it has been formed by heredity and environment. O'Hara's most memorable creations—Julian English, Joe Chapin, Grace and Sidney Tate, who inhabit O'Hara's best work or portions of it—all behave as they must. Their behavior may not be predictable, but it is almost always credible. Conversely, O'Hara's lesser fictions are populated by incompletely visualized characters; and, while O'Hara's narrative skill is sufficient to carry the reader along, once the tale ends the reader's questions begin.

So it is with *The Big Laugh.* Every major development in the novel's action derives from some sudden or profound alteration in a character's behavior. The fundamental change, that on which the entire novel depends, is that of Hubie Ward from scoundrel to solid citizen to scoundrel once more. Unfortunately, however, only the first and supposedly "true" phase of Hubie's conduct receives detailed treatment. Apparently the middle stage permits nothing vivid because of the very nature of respectability; aside from a single brief fling with a French leading lady in one of his films, Hubie leads the sober, faithful, restrained life of any ambitious executive. But we can never fully believe Hubie's conversion to the path of virtue because as one of O'Hara's demonic people, he is so disposed toward evil he must have been born to it. By the time he leaves his teens, Hubie has been dismissed from three prep schools (one for enjoying the attentions of a homosexual schoolmate, another for compromising the wife of the school dentist); killed an old woman during a joyride in his uncle's car (borrowed without permission); despoiled any number of virgins (including the daughter of his mother's only close friend); and committed uncountable other cruel, careless, or criminal deeds. He is also capable of larceny and blackmail. And he has done all this with little guilt or remorse. Only O'Hara's sardonically humorous depiction of the early and presumably basic Hubie Ward saves the character from the reader's utter loathing and contempt.

Could such a person become the pillar of respectability later portrayed? Although the writer does announce at the novel's outset that Hubie's reformation was never more than temporary and superficial, it was at least deep and lasting enough to fool a great many people, including the woman who married him and including Hubie himself. Indeed, Hubie plays the part of respectability so well that his wife begins an extra-marital dalliance out of sheer boredom with her once-intriguing husband. One also wonders what has happened to the resentment and sense of alienation which had purportedly driven Hubie to his earlier anti-social acts (O'Hara explains this by reference to Hubie's shame for his father, an embezzler and suicide). Could the Hubie who, at the age of twenty, believes the world and its people are plums to be picked for his own delectation become dependable and nice before he reached thirty—especially when confronted daily by the succession of glittering depravities accessible to the movie star?

The same sort of question could be posed regarding three other major characters in the novel, Nina Stephens and Mildred and Charley Simmons; but this particular line of inquiry needs no continuation. Even O'Hara's most sympathetic and admiring readers, among whom the present writer numbers himself, must confess that the novelist's fictional people in *The Big Laugh* provoke too many such queries.

The second problem, the characters' power to evoke reader response and identification, is of course related to the matter of their credibility. However, the issue not only has its own integrity, it also bears directly upon the entire Broadway-Hollywood phase of O'Hara's work. To say simply that the cast of *The Big Laugh* and the many other show business types in O'Hara's stories, novels, and plays are low-life characters, and that one does not find such people interesting, is the individual reader's prerogative. However, as O'Hara himself has demonstrated in the creation of Pal Joey (one of Hubie Ward's ancestors) and also in other stories, a character need not be good or even "significant" to be interesting, memorable, or instructive.

What art does require is the author's deep involvement with his own creations. Even when the writer experiences conflicting attitudes and emotions toward his characters, the conflict itself can be the source of life and passion—so long as the artist structures and disciplines his conflict sufficiently to project it into character and action. Above all, he must *feel;* and it is exactly in such feeling O'Hara falls short of the mark. Unfortunately, the characters in *The Big Laugh* and the vast majority of those in O'Hara's other work of this genre seem to exist largely as objects of the author's disdain. The necessary esthetic distance between the author and his characters becomes too great; it produces remoteness rather than objectivity. Even more destructive to the esthetic effect is the impression that the author looks down upon his characters from above. Thus, in his Broadway-Hollywood fiction O'Hara sometimes appears to be amused and sometimes contemptuous, but only rarely engaged. Because ultimately these people usually bore and repel him, or so he leads us to infer, they inevitably bore and repel the reader.

This deduction has already been partially documented, but another sort of evidence exists which cannot be transmitted by quotations and specific references: that implicit in the writer's *tone,* in the sound of his narrative voice rather than in the voice's specific utterance. There is a different *tone* in O'Hara's Broadway-Hollywood work than in his Pennsylvania stories; and, while such an inference might at first seem capricious and subjective, it grows inescapably upon anyone who reads O'Hara carefully. (Not only does one hear it in *The Big Laugh, Hope of Heaven,* and the stories and the plays about show business people, but one hears it occasionally in O'Hara's drama and movie reviews for *Newsweek* and in his review-gossip columns for *Collier's.*) Most often in his fiction O'Hara speaks of these people as one does about laboratory specimens, to be studied with fascinated disgust but only rarely to be taken seriously as forms of life. One might even speculate, finally, that the tone hints at something in O'Hara himself, that it is a means of self-castigation and self-purgation; for, of all O'Hara's major experience, his Broadway-Hollywood years have produced the material of least benefit to his career.

CHAPTER 5

The Short Stories

OVER THE YEARS John O'Hara has published more than three hundred and fifty short stories. These range in length from the one-page *New Yorker* monologues of the late 1920's to the *novellas* included in such recent volumes as *The Cape Cod Lighter* and *The Hat on the Bed*; they also vary in quality from the trivial, slick, and mechanically facile to the profound, serious, and artistically accomplished. In any case, O'Hara's attainments in the short story form are large enough to justify careful attention.

Considering the great bulk of his writing in this genre, O'Hara's performance displays remarkable consistency. Even his poorer collections contain several memorable tales, and in such recent volumes as *The Cape Cod Lighter,* more than half the stories achieve distinction. Moreover, in his stories O'Hara breaks free of most of the faults damaging to his novels: prolixity, verbosity, ambiguity, unconvincing character motivation. In the main his shorter fictions are economical to the point of austerity, thoroughly realistic, wholly credible.

I *The Earlier Stories*

O'Hara matured as a short-story writer early in his career. Although his efforts during the first three or four years were largely satirical monologues of the sort popularized by Sinclair Lewis, Ring Lardner, and Dorothy Parker, O'Hara quickly passed beyond his early parodies of the pompous and hypocritical members of the "Orange County Delphian Society" and the "Idlewood Country Club" and ventured into deeper waters.[1] The satirical monologue continued to be one of his favorite techniques for the exposure of prejudice, folly, and ignorance; however, his first collection, *The Doctor's Son and Other Stories* (1935), indicates that O'Hara had already come upon the basic methods and materials which still characterize his short stories. There have since been important developments and modifications, of course, but in *The Doctor's Son* one hears the voice that no sophisticated reader could mistake for any other.

Almost without exception the stories in *The Doctor's Son* are sensibility stories. Following the example of Chekhov, who has been the greatest single influence upon the course of the modern short story (although O'Hara himself need not have read Chekhov directly, since the same influence was at work upon such writers as Katherine Mansfield, Joyce, and Hemingway), O'Hara's works here depend almost entirely upon character and situation rather than upon plot and action. In fact, many of them are plotless; almost nothing happens. The "action" consists of an entirely different process than that usually denoted by the word. In the sensibility story the action is largely psychological; it arises out of the interplay of the personalities and characters of the story's people. Its climax ordinarily depends far less upon circumstance or other material cause than upon the sudden realization, either by the protagonist or by the audience, of some hitherto unknown or hidden aspect of human nature, more often than not an ugly or unpleasant aspect. This moment of truth, or moment of confrontation of the truth, Joyce called an "epiphany." Likewise, O'Hara's stories often create the effect of what might be called "perceptual distance," or the difference between reality as the story's protagonist views it (or once viewed it) and as the reader, from his superior vantage place and with his superior information, knows it actually to be. The mood or response created by this distance is that of irony, and irony is indeed the effect of virtually every story in *The Doctor's Son,* as it is also generally characteristic of the sensibility story.[2]

This irony may function in two ways. In its most familiar application O'Hara operates as a comic writer and a satirist by aligning himself with the reader and with commonly accepted standards *against* the fictional character; he thus makes the character and his behavior the objects of ridicule and punishment. What O'Hara aims at in such stories have traditionally been the targets for the satirist's shafts: snobbery, viciousness, ostentation, self-importance, conformity; and it is to O'Hara's credit that he riddles human follies and pretensions with savage effectiveness. If O'Hara's satirical stories are not his most profound work—although they lack nothing in cleverness and subtlety—the fault is less O'Hara's than that of satire itself. By its very nature satire forestalls profundity because profundity inhibits the immediate response which satire wishes to arouse.

The first kind of irony, the satirical form, characterizes the majority of stories in *The Doctor's Son,* as it is also prevalent in O'Hara's short fiction written during the 1930's and 1940's. Inverately, O'Hara's aim is to demonstrate that men are not so good as they think themselves, or that their true motives are quite other than those they confess. Such pieces as "Ella and the Chinee," "On His Hands," and "The Girl Who Had Been Presented" set forth savagely comic satirical portraits of egotists who sacrifice others to their own supposedly superior selves, but in truth they are inferior to those they reject or despise.

Other stories, for example "It Wouldn't Break Your Arm," present strikingly accurate satirical likenesses of certain types, in this case the vindictive ex-wife who under the guise of friendship conveys a disturbing piece of information to her recently divorced husband. Occasionally O'Hara plays a variation upon his satirical technique, especially in the monologue, by presenting in an inflated eulogistic style the lives of nonentities whom the eulogist wishes to exalt to heroic stature. This is a type of hyperbole, a mock hyperbole: the trivial and mundane rendered even more trivial by the attempt to dignify and elevate it. Such tales, "Walter T. Carriman" and "Mrs. Whitman" in *Pipe Night,* are especially notable for what they suggest of the tensions, failures, and defeats which the eulogists attempt to gloss over. Once more the result is comic irony, particularly poignant and subtle because it is double-edged in its exposure of both the eulogized and the eulogizer.

There is a sub-species of O'Hara's work in this ironic vein which one hesitates to call "satire" because the comic element has vanished. This species might be labeled "Portraits of Heels," although the word "heel" fails to properly convey the relentless thoroughness of O'Hara's depiction. Such portraits are most common in O'Hara's Broadway-Hollywood fiction, but are by no means limited to it. For example, two of the best stories in *Hellbox* depict superficially different but fundamentally similar men. "Someone to Trust" concerns a small-time mobster, in hiding from his former associates, who bends a trusting ex-girl friend to his purposes by expertly and coldbloodedly playing upon her generosity and sentimentality. "Wise Guy" is a skillful constructed tale wherein the narrator incriminates himself by both word and deed. Separated from his son by divorce, he first forgets and then violates an occasion of reunion with the boy in order to keep a date with one of his female chums. Any concern with the child's feelings occurs to the father only as an irritation.

A female of this same species appears in "Olive" (*Files on Parade*), a sardonic tale about a hotel switchboard operator whose built-in sense of social inferiority expresses itself in the deliberate destruction of a budding and tender relationship between a spinster and an elderly man. These despicable characters all have reason for what they do, but there is a surplus of savagery in them, a gratuitous viciousness not explicable as an outcome of their need to survive; and this sort of malice O'Hara hates and makes his object. Whatever one may call these stories, "satire" no longer seems the proper name.

Actually, the portraits of heels occupy a transitional position between O'Hara's two basic modes of irony. The second kind, the irony inherent in the nature of human nature or the conditions of life or the workings of fate, functions in fewer stories of *The Doctor's Son* and the other collections; but such stories are the more serious and memorable. While in the satiric tales the reader aligned himself with the world against the fictional character, in the stories concerned with irony of character and circumstance the writer wishes to disclose some hard truth about the way things are, to lay bare some secret we once knew but have almost managed to forget, to bring to light some buried facet of character. In these stories the fundamental irony is that inherent in the human condition, the irony of sensitive creatures with ideals and illusions existing in a universe in which the ideal appears only accidentally, if at all, and never for very long. But O'Hara is not at any point "philosophical" or "cosmic"; he avoids such abstractions. Always he works with people, and only with people.

To come to cases, in "The Doctor's Son," the first and longest story in O'Hara's earliest collection, there are two ironic developments: first, that disease kills haphazardly, so that the good often die while the evil flourish; second, that the pressures which ought to stimulate the growth of love often stifle it instead. These developments illustrate both the irony of fate acting as a capricious force, and the irony of fate as it alters character. Another story communicating the same sort of irony is "All the Girls He Wanted." In it a young married woman, expecting to be consoled by her best friend about the death of a man she secretly loves, is herself called upon to supply the consolation to the best friend—whom she learns was the dead man's mistress. Yet another is "Straight Pool," wherein a good but insensitive man, distraught by his marital problems, confesses his troubles to the very fellow responsible for them.

Two stories which graphically demonstrate what might be termed the irony of character, that which stems from misjudging or misunderstanding others or one's self being misunderstood, are "Sportsmanship" and "Over the River and Through the Wood." These, with a few others, are the worthiest stories in the volume and, in general, represent the kinds of O'Hara short fiction which will endure. "Sportsmanship" chillingly demonstrates that the quality of mercy does not reside in every human breast: a young man tries to make restitution to his former employer, owner of a poolroom, by returning to work off his debt for money he has stolen; he does fulfill his promise, serving faithfully until the entire sum has been paid back, only to be mutilated for his unforgiven crime.

"Over the River and Through the Wood," another story reflecting unquestionable artistry (how have anthologists missed it?), unforgettably portrays the final defeat of a now aging and almost broken but once rich, attractive, and important man. His defeat stems from his gesture of friendship toward a beautiful, arrogant young woman, a gesture which she in part misconstrues and attributes to his depravity, and a gesture whose motive the reader himself must ponder. In any case, her contemptuous rejection of him annihilates what little remains of his dignity and self-respect.

Failure, defeat, loss, pain, misfortune, cruelty are the themes dominant in O'Hara's better stories. Occasionally one finds such a tale as "I Never Seen Anything Like It" (in which a speakeasy proprietor recounts how his place was burglarized, marveling all the while at the superb smoothness and efficiency of the hoodlums) that is rich with comic humor. And, as has been seen, humor is rarely absent from the satirical portraits and sketches so prominent in O'Hara's early work, although the comic and satiric stories do not lodge most firmly in the memory. The others—those dealing with the terrors of aging, or the conflict between the old and the young, with the tribulations of love, with the lot of the lonely, the outcast, and the suffering—are the tales which affect the reader most deeply.

Representative of this latter group is the strongly autobiographical "The Doctor's Son," already mentioned above, which invites comparison to such early Hemingway pieces as "Indian Camp." Not only is the style Hemingwayesque—its terse sentences indited by the youthful narrator who speaks as if through clenched teeth—but also the theme: a boy's initiation into life and his forced recognition of its agonies. During the influenza epidemic in which Jimmy Malloy acts as a driver both for his overworked doctor-father and for a medical student brought in to assist in this emergency, he learns about disease, death, and deceit. Although as a physician's son in a mining community young Malloy is not unused to death and sickness, the amount here overwhelms him. The atmosphere of disease and unpredictable disaster is further accentuated by what he observes of man's inner corruption, especially the conduct of Mrs. Evans with the young man who has come in to heal and save. Against this background the story poses an ironic counterpoint, that between "Love" (both Mrs. Evans' adulterous love for Dr. Meyers and Jimmy's own pure love for Edith Evans) and Death, which seems to prefer as its victims the good, the strong, the innocent, and the gentle. As a final irony it seems that love, both pure and depraved, is a graveyard flower best nourished by disease and death. Hardly a cheerful or uplifting story, this, but there is nothing trivial about it.

In accord with the predominantly ironic view of his earlier story collections, O'Hara's inquiries into human nature are more likely to sadden than exhilarate. Most frequently he uncovers some wickedness, some depravity, some buried sin, often where one least expects it. A number of stories in *Pipe Night* are among many that could be cited in support of this conclusion. In "On Time" Laura, the story's protagonist, thought a model of virtue and dependability by her friends, regains her lost pride by cruelly lying to her former lover about the circumstances of a crucial rendezvous. Likewise, Kathy in "Too Young," betrays the adoration of her young admirer when he learns that she is cheap enough to take her pleasure with a tough motorcycle cop. Nor is there anything especially admirable about either partner of the decaying marriage portrayed in "Radio." The wife who has deceived her husband invites no more disdain than the nasty-mouthed and petty man she has cuckolded. But no matter how disenchanted O'Hara's perspective in these stories, one never infers misanthropy. There is too much regard for what people suffer. No one who reads such a story as "Now We Know," with its poignant portrayal of a doomed-from-the-start love between a Jewish bus driver and his Irish passenger, a receptionist, could ever suspect O'Hara of the callousness and contempt for humans which is essential to misanthropy. O'Hara is simply a Realist.

Although irony pervades the best stories among those published during the first two decades of O'Hara's career, *The Doctor's Son, Files on Parade, Pipe Night,* and *Hellbox* are all softened and illuminated by a compassion which tempers the irony, keeping it from nihilism and despair. In such pieces as "The Man Who Had to Talk to Somebody," "Alone," "Hotel Kid," and "In the Morning Sun" (all from *The Doctor's Son*), O'Hara reveals his sympathy with the lonely, the outcast, and the suffering: a man who has lost his family and status because of imprisonment for a bad check and yet who does not seek pity, only someone to listen to him when he is compelled to air his misery; a recently widowed husband about to attend burial services for his wife, who has drowned; an intelligent and forelorn little boy who spends his childhood in hotel corridors while his mother, a high-class prostitute, travels from city to city in search of big money; a man of once-compelling mind and personality, exhausted before he is thirty, afflicted by some incalculable and inexpressible inner torment—these are some of the characters and situations which evoke O'Hara's compassionate response. Furthermore, O'Hara's affection and admiration for certain kinds of people stand out in such stories as "Pleasure," in which O'Hara delineates the stern self-discipline of a working girl whose life is lived so close to the bone that her concept of pleasure is to smoke an entire cigarette.

Files on Parade, a collection generally not complimentary to O'Hara because so much of it consists of mere sketches, anecdotes, and vignettes, nevertheless contains two stories which show both O'Hara's compassion and his deep knowledge of human behavior. "The Cold House" is a delicate and moving tale about a woman who travels to her summer house in the attempt to recapture the memory of her son, buried not long before. However, she realizes that if she makes an altar of her grief and a museum of her dead son's possessions, she will soil and pervert her true feelings for him, and so she returns to her own life in the city. A few lines from this story demand citation for what they illustrate of the tautness of O'Hara's prose and the discipline with which he handles emotion:

> She could see clearly, like watching a motion picture of herself, what she would have done, what she had been in terrible danger of doing: next August, next September, a year from next August and a year from next July, she would have come up here, unlocked the door, come in this room and stood. She saw herself, a woman in white, trying to squeeze out a tear at the sight of these things of wood and brass and paper and glass—and all the while distracted by the sounds of passing cars, the children next door, the telephone downstairs, the whirring vacuum cleaner. And she even knew the end of this motion picture: she would end by hating a memory that she only knew how to love.[3]

O'Hara's extraordinary insight into the thoughts and emotions of the old extends as well to his treatment of the minds and hearts of the young. "Do You Like It Here?" deals with the persecution of a new boy at a fashionable prep school by one of the school's resident instructors. The master accuses the student of stealing, a gambit which is but the beginning of a whole process of terrorization which will destroy the boy's life at the school. And because he is the son of divorced parents and has moved from place to place, he lacks the stability of background and record which would make him invulnerable to persecution. An even more ominous undertone sounds if one infers, as the story suggests, that there has been no theft at all and that a sadistic instructor torments his chosen victim for his own perverse pleasure. Yet what could have been a bitter, dead-end tale is made deeply affecting because of O'Hara's involvement in the destiny of his protagonist.

Virtually all of O'Hara's basic techniques of short fiction are exhibited in *The Doctor's Son* and in the other collections between 1935 and 1947. In *The Doctor's Son*, as elsewhere, almost every tale is related by a speaking voice. Sometimes it is the single voice of the story's central character cast in the form of satirical monologue. Sometimes the voice is that of the first-person narrator who may be merely the source of information about the story's protagonist (the "I as Witness" approach) as in "The Man Who Had to Talk to Somebody" and "Hotel Kid"; or the narrator may himself be the central character (the "I as Protagonist"), as in "The Doctor's Son" and in "It Must Have Been Spring." Sometimes one overhears the voice of the protagonist speaking to himself (the interior monologue), as in "It Wouldn't Break Your Arm," "Back in New Haven," and "All the Girls He Wanted." Or O'Hara may combine two points of view, opening in the conventional manner of the editorial omniscient to establish setting and cast, and then subtly shifting into the interior monologue as in "Mrs. Galt and Edwin" and in "In the Morning Sun"—or into dialogue which constitutes the remainder of the story as in "The Girl Who Had Been Presented" and in "On His Hands."

Even when O'Hara employs, as he often does, the editorial omniscient, one has the sense of *listening* to a story rather than seeing it on the page. Description and narration are at a minimum; dialogue is virtually all. Thus, O'Hara's method is the dramatic rather than the panoramic.[4] What we learn from these stories we learn as in life: by watching people behave and listening to them speak. Further, O'Hara has the marvelous gift of constructing exactly the sort of dramatic scene, of catching precisely the tones and shadings and inflections which enable, indeed which require, the reader to grasp the truth. At his best he gives us an unsurpassed sense of reality, of life happening *now*, as if spontaneously.

Another of O'Hara's fundamental and characteristic methods, undoubtedly developed in the short story before being employed in the novels, is that already seen elsewhere: the delayed revelation. In the stories O'Hara makes it serve as the uncovering, usually at the last moment, of some essential fact or happening (often in the character's past) which completes the reader's knowledge of the protagonist and permits him to distinguish between the character's version of reality and reality itself. We watch and listen, learning as the story (and the speaking voice) proceed. We suspect, conjecture, infer until at last we *know*. To O'Hara's credit this delayed revelation is rarely of the sort still employed in the well-made story as it was perfected by O.

Henry; that is, it does not ordinarily involve some new development or unforeseen twist of circumstance. Rather, it is the final and culminating piece of information which impels the reader to complete his conjectures and suspicions, and from them to draw illuminating conclusions.

By this method O'Hara also achieves many of his ironic effects. For example, in "Mary," the story of a beautiful but unlettered Polish girl who rises in the world by dint of her charms and their shrewd dispensation, we perceive what Mary really is (despite her lavish apartment, fashionable address, and imposing manners) in the story's concluding lines: "One night I called her and she had nothing to do, so I went to see her. I was very careful of my behavior, never batting an eye when she said 'eyether,' and drinking my highball in a chair that was a room's width away from her. The telephone rang. She answered it and made a date with the voice at the other end of the wire. She hung up and smiled at me. 'That was Ted Frisbee, the polo-player,' she said. 'I'm awf'ly fond of him. He has such a nice sense of yoomer.'"[5]

As in the passage above, the effect may be satirical, in this case gently and comically so. Elsewhere the revelation may be far more somber, opening up to the reader a vista of anguish already suffered and more pain yet to come. In "In the Morning Sun" a mother watches her twenty-seven year old son who has already been through a destructive divorce, a serious illness, and other possible disasters. As in other such instances of the delayed revelation, this entire story pivots upon a slight action and a few whispered words: "She stood up again and looked out at Sam. He was not reading, he did not look as though he cared or knew whether there was anyone else in the world. When she first looked, he was leaning forward and his hands covered his forehead and temples and eyes, and then his head went back and his tired face faced the sky, and she could almost hear him saying it: 'Oh. Oh.' And his mother shivered, for there was nothing she could do."[6]

From these examples it should be apparent that, while the delayed revelation is essentially a technique, a mode of construction, it also connotes the writer's world-view. Given thematic application and interpretation, the delayed revelation states O'Hara's belief that human beings always retain some mystery concealed to even their most intimate associates, and that the dullest and seemingly most predictable is a creature of infinite variety. Whether or not this is the ultimate truth about people, once the reader enters O'Hara's imagined world, he convinces us that it is so. No mere hack could accomplish this sort of persuasion.

Since O'Hara's expertise as a writer of short stories has often been admired but rarely discussed in detail and almost never subjected to close analysis, a careful study of two representative stories should serve to support some of the conclusions advanced above and to convey a more precise understanding of O'Hara's method. "Radio" (*Pipe Night*) and "Horizon" (*Hellbox*) are characteristic pieces. Both are relatively short, tightly written, and quietly effective; and, although one might hesitate to call them the best of O'Hara, they are certainly typical of the good O'Hara. Both also illustrate the pervasive irony of O'Hara's earlier stories.

"Horizon" employs that point-of-view which O'Hara does peculiarly well: the editorial omniscient which merges into the interior monologue. While the surface of the story remains consistently third person, with O'Hara and the reader seemingly viewing the characters from outside, with the characters referred to by name or third-person pronoun, and with verbs cast in the past tense, actually O'Hara works much of the time from inside the protagonist's mind to apprise the reader of hidden truths no observer could know. As a result, the reader—without realizing just how and when—moves from the vantage place of third person to first person, from outside to inside.

Strictly speaking, this is not interior monologue of the Proustian or Joycean sort because one does not get the complete impression of participating in thoughts at the very instant of their formulation, of being borne on a stream of sensual responses, of hearing the inchoate and incessant flow of silent speech uttered in the brain. O'Hara can achieve this impression also, and he does employ the classic interior monologue on occasion, as in the story "Alone" (*The Doctor's Son*); but, much more characteristically, he conjoins the finished and conclusive effect derived from the objective mode with the immediate and concrete effect of the subjective.

A citation from "Horizon" should illustrate how observations which could come only from the outside are intermingled with those which could only be originated by the protagonist. Although I have italicized only those few lines which O'Hara casts strictly in the form of interior monologue, in actuality it would be extraordinarily difficult for the reader to distinguish between what the character is thinking and what the author is observing. Shortly after the story begins, its protagonist—McGuire, a longtime newspaperman—gazes out his office window and meditates upon his past:

> For eighteen years this side of the state capitol had been his horizon. *Well, that was not precisely true.* He had only been sitting at a desk facing the city room, and beyond it, this side of the capitol ten years—about ten years. There had been the times he had sat in on the night desk, when his horizon was the mailboxes and newspaper files. *You could take those times out of the eighteen years. You could also take out the four months* when he had undergone a miserable self-imposed exile as managing editor of the *Beacon.** The *Beacon** being on Front Street, he hadn't even seen the capitol dome. At the Beacon his horizon had been Holzheimer's Storage Warehouse—Long Distance Moving. But anyway, to all intents and purposes he was now looking at what had been his horizon for either ten or eighteen years. *Either way it was no good, and eighteen was only a little worse than ten. You didn't get used to hanging if you hung long enough.* With some bitterness McGuire reflected that hoodlums could have painted dirty words on the other side of the state capitol, or a strange art commission could have painted it with pink and blue diagonal stripes, and he wouldn't have known about it. Oh, he'd have *heard** about it, and most likely in the case of a story as important as that he would have done the rewrite job on it. But in the ordinary course of his life, he would not have seen the words or the stripes.[7]

By such simple yet expert methods does O'Hara attain the effect of simultaneity and depth.

The passage above contains yet other evidence of the subtlety of O'Hara's approach. This excerpt from the second paragraph of the story already conveys something of the desolation, loneliness, and emotional poverty of McGuire's life. That is the very crux of the story, as well as its ironic point, for McGuire invites comparison with such other tormented souls as Melville's Bartleby. Indeed, McGuire with his fixed view of the wall of the state capitol, with his profession as a kind of scrivener, and with

* O'Hara's italics.

his inability to engage in deeply meaningful interchange with other humans reminds the reader of Bartleby; but McGuire is a more verbal and familiar figure. If O'Hara hardly equals Melville's enormous genius, his more limited aims are admirably executed. Suspicious of metaphor and not a symbolist in any wide sense of the term, O'Hara does capably employ emblems to underscore his meaning. Thus in the passage just cited there are a series of ironic wordplays and cunning juxtapositions which underlie O'Hara's seemingly transparent prose and intensify the story's theme and impact.

The first and most obvious of the ironic devices is the wordplay involved in the contrast between the word "horizon"—the leitmotif of the passage and the title of the story, with all it suggests of distance, vastness, hope, possibility—and such other words as "desk," "city room" (in itself an ironic combination), "mailboxes," "files," *Front* Street" (my italics), and "storage warehouse.' A second ironic implication is the notion that such a man as McGuire once managed a newspaper called the *Beacon*, with all it connotes of illumination, freedom, inquiry, idealism; and, even more ironic, McGuire found his employment there "a miserable self-imposed exile."

A third ironic device is O'Hara's contrast of McGuire's present existence with the two buildings whose exteriors McGuire knows better than any others and whose walls he has come to think of as a sort of prison, the state capitol and the storage warehouse. Although much that goes on in a state capitol is dull, much of it is also momentous, involving decisions and crises affecting multitudes of people. Similarly, a storage warehouse does not on first thought seem a very stimulating place; but, when one realizes that this is the warehouse of a long-distance moving company and that the objects it contains have been heaped up by the constant flux and change which are the backwash of modern life, one sees again demonstrated that lack of imagination, that unwillingness or inability to unleash the heart and mind which are precisely McGuire's defects and which in fact constitute his "self-imposed exile."

Further, in his visualization of such events as the defacement of the state capitol by "hoodlums" or its adornment by a "strange art commission" one perceives McGuire's conceptualization of any lapse from the routine as distasteful. These thoughts are a final insight into McGuire's mental patterns. But what prevents him from simply walking around to look at the other side of the state capitol, or from taking a different and longer way to work? McGuire could supply no answers to such questions, other than that it never occurred to him to do so, or that it was too much trouble. Only chance or some special assignment could propel him out of his customary path. Because the reader knows this, because O'Hara has made him know it, he realizes that McGuire will never carry out his sudden impulse to quit his job and strike out for new horizons. One realizes, too, that McGuire's greatest adventure will be the mere contemplation of the idea of quitting, of shattering the mold. In this fashion O'Hara combines in "Horizon" ironic technique with irony of theme. Withal, the story leaves no corrosive taste upon the reader's palate because O'Hara not only presents McGuire but also *judges* him with mercy and concern.

Like many O'Hara stories, "Radio" is written in the editorial omniscient mode, but most of the tale actually consists of dialogue. All narration and description are kept at an absolute minimum. The work opens with three short expository sentences setting the scene and identifying the main characters, and from time to time there are other extremely brief narrative passages, stage directions really, interposed to provide continuity. In fact, because all but a hundred words of the story are dialogue, it could with very little revision be staged as an exceedingly compact but complete one-act play.

Since the dialogue must carry such heavy weight, taking upon itself the burdens usually borne by narration, description, and exposition, it must be totally convincing and representative of its speakers; and it is. The speakers are a badly educated man and wife of lower middle class. However, they are neither obtuse nor grossly ignorant. They have that hard practical intelligence, that keen functional awareness, that capacity for double-meanings, insinuations, and repartee which is true both of a particular kind of person and of one type of standard O'Hara character. In any case, the writer, who depicts them with unchallengeable fidelity, discerns just the right grammatical errors, slang and catch-phrases, constructions and locutions, to set them perfectly as to class and background. More profoundly, he conveys that mixture of ignorance and knowledge, that pretense of sophisticated cynicism adopted in order to disguise basic confusion, which characterize an intellect in quasi-developed condition. For example, there is this discussion of popularity polls:

> She rubbed her lower lip. "I wonder who they call up and ask them what they're listening to. They never asked me. I don't even know anybody they ever asked."
>
> "That's not the way they do it anymore. They have another way of doing it nowadays."
>
> "How do they, then?" she said.
>
> "Well, they still use the phone in some cases. In certain cases they call up and ask you what program are you listening to, but then they have other ways too."
>
> "*What* other ways?"
>
> "Why, they take some kind of a cross section of the public—what income bracket you're in, how many cars do you own, how many radios and so on, and they figure out how many people are listening to such-and-such a program."
>
> "How could they figure it out if they didn't ask you?"
>
> "They don't have to ask each individual party. They have their own way of doping it out from some kind of a formula. Naturally they don't go around blabbing what the formula is, or otherwise why couldn't I steal the formula and go into business for myself with their idea?"
>
> "In other words, you don't know."
>
> "Of course I don't know. I never pretended as if I did know."
>
> "Oh, no, certainly not. If I wouldn't of asked you a simple question like how did they figure it out you would of gone on all night talking like a big authority on the subject, and wouldn't that be typical."[8]

Such painfully comic and superbly accurate rendition of marital bickering comprises most of the story, and from this sample one can understand why certain critics have claimed that O'Hara could not write his dialogue but must catch it instead on some recording device. But there is another than linguistic dimension. The passage just cited also transmits something of the motivation, of the very quality, of each of the marital partners. He is pompous and verbally self-assertive as a cover for his essential sense of inferiority. She is wholly pragmatic, impressed only by demonstrated results. One suspects that she continually leads her husband into such traps precisely so as to gain further opportunities to undercut him—opportunities she would never bypass. Deeper yet, it is likely that her husband's bluster but fundamental ineffectuality as a man (an ineffectuality she pro-

mulgates by her castration techniques) have allowed her, perhaps even impelled her, to seek gratification outside of marriage
with a man formerly their friend, a man we also infer has the
charm and daring her husband lacks.

However, the wife's adultery is not revealed until the last
twenty lines of the story; and once revealed, the couple's irrita-
bility with one another, the sarcastic edge of each remark, and
the tangible atmosphere of tension and hostility suddenly leap
into new and sharper perspective. The reader had attributed
the bickering to the kind of incompatibility, the contempt bred
by familiarity, the consistent mediocrity common to many (the
cynic would say *most*) marriages. The husband's role becomes
especially coherent, for he has learned of his wife's misbehavior
without her awareness of his special knowledge. This knowledge
has given him the upper hand in the marriage, for the first time
one suspects; and, ironically true to his wife's conception of him,
his new role only intensifies his arrogance. Yet, to her surprise,
his arrogance is now no longer mere bluster. With the realization
that he has been cuckolded, Klauser becomes a man—or, more
accurately, a male. If this is not to say he becomes a whole
human being, at least he discovers enough nerve in his sense of
his wife's vulnerability to take command of the cave, for the
present. And so the story ends, as Klauser confronts his wife
with her misdeed and simultaneously assumes mastery:

> He got up and went to her. "Thinking of the children all of
> a sudden, eh? How about at Rockaway, those times you and
> Harry—I guess you were thinking about the children then? And
> a couple of other times I could mention I'm not suppose to know
> about." He slapped her hard across the face. "You bitch."
> "Don't you hit me again," she said.
> "Sure I will," he said, and did. "As much as I want to,
> because, Baby, you're stuck." He walked to a taboret where he
> kept his rye. He took out a pint bottle and held it up to the
> light. He began to sing softly: "Da-da de da-da de da. 'Don't
> get around much any more.' Baby, are you stuck!"
> She nodded. "Uh-huh," she said. "I'm stuck."9

With this exchange of sarcasms, as each character makes his
separate plans for the future and the reader enjoys a multiple
awareness of the ironic possibilities inherent in the situation,
O'Hara wins through to one of his most admirable effects: a

sense of the ongoing current of existence. Whatever happens between Klauser and his wife, their lives can never be as they were. The ultimate irony is that each is "stuck" with the other; that, if Klauser continues to play the overlord, he will lose all remaining chances for serenity. So, too, the wife must realize that she can neither go back to her former status as loyal spouse nor on to other lovers without surrendering the shards of her self-respect.

These ironies of characterization and theme are emphasized and counterpointed by the story's deployment of language. The entire conversation which ends in the revelation and crisis stems from the song "Don't Get Around Much Any More," broadcast over the radio in what at first appears to be a cosy domestic scene. The husband hears the song, comments upon it, one remark engenders another, until finally the words of the refrain, "don't get around much any more," are turned back upon the wife in Klauser's exposure of her infidelity. There is yet other ironic wordplay. Throughout the story we note the stress upon and repetition of such words as "funny" and "laugh," underscoring this hardly humorous situation. The word "radio" also recurs, signifying the dehumanized quality of the couple's relationship. Perhaps the most telling technique of all, which cannot be fully described but only named, is O'Hara's skill in arranging all the seemingly random, disjointed, and offhand remarks of this apparently routine marital bickering into a subtle and tightly woven pattern delineating the texture of two lives. With all its swerves, irrelevancies, and circumlocutions, the dialogue drives swiftly and powerfully to its intended goal. It recalls similar treatments by Chekhov of the dreariness of many common lives.[10]

II *The Later Stories*

After *Hellbox* (1947) no new collection of O'Hara stories appeared for thirteen years, his big novels occupying most of his attention during that period. Then, as he relates in his foreword to *Assembly* (1960), O'Hara resumed his work in the short story with the joyful discovery that he had an almost unlimited flow of short-story ideas waiting for expression.[11] In the past few years three other volumes have been issued, *The Cape Cod Lighter* (1962), *The Hat on the Bed* (1964), and *The Horse Knows the*

Way (1964). With *Assembly* they leave no doubt that in this later phase O'Hara is an even more mature and accomplished craftsman than in his earlier volumes.

The stories in *Assembly* and in the other recent collections, though longer, display no major technical innovation or development. There may be some verbosity in the later works, and their pace is decidedly more leisurely, but more often than not the greater length results from the amplified dimensions, density, and solidity of the situations O'Hara selects. Furthermore, there is far less of the mere facility that often marred the stories of the 1930's and 1940's.

While O'Hara's methods remain relatively constant, they are employed with increased sureness. All but a few of the later stories use the omniscient mode; the rest are written from the viewpoint of first-person narrator. They utilize a straight chronological approach, avoid stylistic or structural innovations, and depend heavily upon dialogue; in them, narration and exposition serve mainly as a frame. The prose is effortless, lucid, direct. The dominant structural and psychological strategy continues to be that of the delayed revelation. Most of the stories can still be classified as sensibility stories, and none counts heavily upon twists and turns of plot.

Despite the increased length of the later tales, many are so terse and economical that the reader must follow with the utmost care, for an entire story might hinge upon a single bit of dialogue, a single detail. So, for example, in *The Hat on the Bed* the effect of "Saturday Lunch" arises from the unconscious irony of the husbands' casual observation that their wives are "delicate," when in fact the malaise of the two women springs from their mutual secret and from fear of further molestation by the sex deviate who has accosted them both. The car salesman's suicidal despair in "How Can I Tell You" is both foreshadowed and explicated by his seemingly cryptic and disjointed remarks about undertakers: "Every business is the same," and "We're all in it for the money." The theme of "The Golden" resides in the story's underplayed but crucial suggestion of the similarity between people and dogs. Moreover, these nuances set forth the conflict of values inherent in each situation: the women in "Saturday Lunch" who would rather risk physical harm and despoilment than the possibility of scandal; the car salesman in "How Can I Tell You" for whom the making of money is no longer enough to sustain life and sanity;

the mother in "The Golden" who realizes bitterly that her properly reared daughter would willingly trade respectability, duty, and good taste for the indulgence of her romantic and sexual whims.

The prime difference between the stories issuing out of the first two decades of O'Hara's career and those of recent vintage is therefore not that in technique. Rather, the later stories are characterized by different emphases in mood, situation, and theme. If *irony* could be called the dominant characteristic of the early tales, then *compassion* must be named as typical of the later. In other words, there has been a reversal of emphasis.

To turn first to *Assembly*, one notes that perhaps its most remarkable aspect is O'Hara's concern with age. Of the volume's twenty-six stories at least half are either wholly involved with the experience of aging and the consciousness of impending death, or have as their central character a person of middle age or older. During his eleven-year absence from the short-story form, O'Hara had suffered deep personal tragedy. Just a few months after being himself stricken by a near-fatal illness, he was shocked by the death of his beloved wife, Belle. Hence, an autumnal mood pervades *Assembly* as well as most of O'Hara's recent work, a mood sharply in contrast with the predominantly caustic and ironic tone of the earlier collections.[12]

Nevertheless he refuses to sentimentalize what in the hands of a popular writer quickly becomes a cloying subject; rather, O'Hara's treatment is tough-minded and realistic. His aging and old people are as they have lived; the passage of time in itself has made them neither more saintly nor more sinful. If they become wise and good, they do so only as they have lived wise and good lives. Nor, to recognize the converse stereotype which O'Hara avoids, are his old people crotchety, feeble, and repulsive simply because they are old.

The characters' chief problem derives from the omnipresence of death and the heightened moral awareness stimulated by it. Again and again in these stories the reader is reminded in a completely credible and unsensational manner that in late middle age the heart may simply stop functioning as one drives an automobile ("Reassurance") or while one plays cards with friends ("The Trip"). The body does not become loathsome, it merely becomes unreliable; and, if it has been punished by overwork, excessive strain, or alcohol, one can count on it all the less. To some degree it retains its appetites, but they are no longer so urgent; if they are to be gratified, they must be gratified in a seemly and disciplined fashion. Only the elderly man or woman who abrogates the dignity and responsibility of age invokes O'Hara's contempt, as in his biting depiction of the coarse actress in "The Man with the Broken Arm" and of the elderly homosexual in "The Sharks."

However, O'Hara concerns himself less with the body than with the condition of the mind and spirit. To O'Hara the waning years are a time for reassessment and reappraisal, for a full and final inquiry into the quality of one's life as that quality has been determined by decisions long made and long sustained. Especially in affairs of the heart does old age offer the final test of choices made in youth. So in such memorable stories as "The Compliment" and "The Properties of Love" lovers once more meet after a span of years to review bygone intimacies, or are returned by their memories to the moment of choice. Friends now, passion replaced by tenderness, they speak at last the truth: of the wrong mate chosen, of the surrender to circumstance, of the head's sway over the heart. They regret the lost happiness which might have been theirs, but they usually regret without rancor or recrimination, for each has found a way to survive and each has won through to acceptance, if not peace.

In these stories one often discovers an even greater tribute to the power of love than in those dealing with the affections of younger men and women who can still alter their lives. Or, to be more precise, O'Hara pays homage to the *stamina* of love, which prevails over obstacles and persists through time, distance, and absence. At the same time, when love confronts a moral crisis, as in "The Lighter When Needed" and in "You Can Always Tell Newark," the lovers of O'Hara's recent depiction often possess enough conviction in the purity of their feeling for another to surrender their desires for the sake of decency. Certainly they pay for their ethics heavily in loneliness, misery, and frustration, but out of their travail they sometimes take a brightened and ultimately more serene self. Whatever their sufferings, the single or married life they build apart from the first and always most joyous love is infinitely cleaner, infinitely preferable to the sordid adulteries O'Hara portrays in such other stories as "Mary and Norma" and "The Free."

This capacity to love, as strong in age as in youth, constitutes one of O'Hara's most affirmative statements, whether the love be for a lost sweetheart ("The High Point") or for a child gone wrong ("Mrs. Stratton of Oak Knoll"). The conclusion to the latter story could well stand as the summation of a theme recurrent in his later work. In it a very old woman, once rich and proud, faces the end of her life with the awful knowledge that both her children are degenerate failures, and yet she asks her neighbor: " 'Tell me, Mr. Reese, so wise and kind you are, why does *this* last?' She held her hand to her bosom. 'Something must,' he said."[13]

It seems a paradox that while roughly half the stories in *Assembly* relate either to love or age or both, the other half concern rogues, scoundrels, heels, bitches, cheats, "queers," and the driven, the tormented, and the depraved. However, what seems a paradox is not completely so, for in these tales O'Hara's underlying concern is still moral; his people and their actions continue to be set against unwavering standards. Only one story, the bizarre but compelling "In a Grove," might be open to the charge of sensationalism—of sex and violence for their own sake; yet as we reread the story and ponder it, we see that the ruthless and at first shocking killings at the tale's conclusion have been carefully foreshadowed and persuasively motivated. Therefore, while O'Hara certainly does not condone the murderer's actions—his cold ferocity is unspeakable—he does render his behavior intelligible. Similarly, in "The Free" the story concludes with the promise of violence to come, its motivation identical to that of "In a Grove:" one man's transgression against the privacy of another's marriage.

In fact, never in O'Hara's fiction has "the case against adultery" been clearer or more emphatic. From the pampered *nouveau-riche* slut who sleeps with waiters ("Sterling Silver"), to the ex-prizefighter compelled to parade his masculinity at the cost of his newly acquired respectability ("The Weakness"), to the two promiscuous middle-class wives ("Mary and Norma"), O'Hara presents a panorama of moral defectives. Yet O'Hara's methods are so deft, his style so understated, that one searches in vain for the author's own *pronounced* judgment. All is objectified, O'Hara himself never intruding to editorialize. At his most obvious, he does no more than insert other characters whose moral vision the reader can equate with the author's, as in "Sterling Silver."

To O'Hara's further accomplishment as a Realist, his sinners do not fall upon their knees in penitence. People being what they are, O'Hara suggests, they will find ways to excuse themselves or, failing that, simply remain defiant. Accordingly, the two wives (who are also sisters-in-law) in "Mary and Norma" justify their infidelities by despising their boorish and insensitive husbands and by agreeing that the fault must be shared not only by their mates but by all males: " 'I wonder if they hate us as much,' said Mary. 'If they didn't, we wouldn't be talking this way.' 'I guess not.' "[14] Even more hardened is Charles D'Avlon of "Exactly Eight Thousand Dollars, Exactly," a packed story which examines the qualities of two lives, those of a good and an evil brother. Nearing sixty now but still undaunted, Charles continues as he always has, abusing, exploiting, hurting, but always escaping the consequences. Because he does not care what others think of him, he is immune to reprisal. Furthermore, he still retains his two keenest weapons: his charm, irresistible when he wishes it to be; and his ability to intuit the weakness of others and humiliate them by word or act. Even with his back to the wall when he comes to his good, successful brother for money and is forced to listen to an unsparing indictment, Charles remains unregenerate. Yet, although the distance between moralist and evangelist is not very far in this story, O'Hara is the better writer for not crossing it.

As one surveys the range of O'Hara's recent short fiction, the Charles D'Avlons are decidedly in the minority. Much more often O'Hara deals with the lonely, the outcast, the suffering, or with those drowning in a sea of boredom and triviality. Such lives had always been of interest to O'Hara, and one finds a story or two about them in almost every collection—but never so many as in the later work. *The Cape Cod Lighter,* a consistently praiseworthy volume, contains six such tales as well as a number of others recounting the fortunes of those afflicted by the tribulations of love or ravaged by old mistakes.

Four of them, perhaps the collection's best, serve to illustrate this point. All focus on people whose lives have lost something precious: either the hopes and dreams of youth, as in "The Father"; fame and the respect of others, as in "The First Day"; the zest and satisfaction of day-to-day existence, as in "Sunday Morning"; or independence and self-respect, as in "Money." The protagonist of "The First Day" is a once-famous journalist who, because of his weakness for alcohol and other defects we can only surmise, has returned to a job on the same small-city paper where he had begun his career. The major characters in the other three stories are all much more ordinary: a lower-middle class working man, a suburban housewife, an aging spinster.

By some small act or combination of acts these characters are brought painfully to an insight into their lives, an epiphany, when suddenly they become aware that the illusions, ideals, and satisfactions which once sustained them no longer hold true. Poignantly, with the understated tragic sense of the Realist, O'Hara presents them as they confront the bleak emptiness of their conditions: the working man reminded of the brightness of his youth by an old photograph, of a time when he spoke exuberantly rather than with the disgruntled snarl typical of his middle age; the newsman who once hobnobbed with the great and shaped the opinions of millions, now conscious that he has become such a bore he cannot hold another man's attention for the duration of a conversation over lunch; the housewife whose home, husband, children, and routine are, one Sunday morning, no longer enough for happiness, no longer enough even for the pretense of happiness; the once sturdily self-sufficient and keen-minded woman who, without knowing or realizing quite how or when, has allowed herself to be dominated by her sister and her circumstances just at the time when her own comfortable income should bring her a fuller, freer life. Nor does O'Hara, consistent with his world view, suggest easy solutions or single out simplistic causes for these conditions.

If *The Hat on the Bed* and if *The Horse Knows the Way* (both published in 1964) can be taken as a prediction or promise of work to come, the reader has much more to expect from O'Hara in the short story. Certainly his most recent efforts indicate that the temporary retirement from story writing which he announces in his foreword to the latter volume has not been forced by infirmity. The work in *The Horse Knows the Way* asserts, rather, that O'Hara can still surprise with his vigor and originality. For example, one suspects that the latter-day phase or mood of compassion may in the future be overshadowed by a renewed emphasis upon the violent, the grim, and the negative since eighteen of these twenty-eight stories record some kind of demise, defeat, deterioration—although of a different sort than in the early collections.

O'Hara's method also escapes complete predictability. "The Bonfire," on its surface a lucidly matter-of-fact narrative about the adjustment problems of a young widow, is charged with strong symbolic undercurrents. O'Hara has never written a better closing scene for a story than in this one, which finds the woman near her summer home on the beach at night, under the stars, in the darkness, between the sea and a bonfire. And exquisite craft of a different nature is embodied in the subtle foreshadowing and delicately balanced structure of "The Madeline Wherry Case."

After these and other admirable examples of O'Hara's short fiction, one greets with mixed feelings his announcement that he is returning to what he apparently considers a higher calling, the novel. One speculates whether O'Hara will be able to attain such consistently high quality in the longer form; but, on the basis of his previous record, there seems little cause for doubt.

CHAPTER 6

A Summary and Assessment

JUDGMENTS OF O'HARA, favorable and otherwise, have not been wanting in the preceding pages of this study. It should be plain that he is a flawed writer. But, before coming to a final assessment and a statement of his virtues, it is necessary to register three complaints not heretofore emphasized. The first concerns O'Hara's public utterances. The second has to do with O'Hara as thinker. The third pertains to one aspect of O'Hara's technique.

Whenever O'Hara speaks in his own voice directly to the reader, as he has frequently done in his prefaces and forewords and in his journalistic writings (in the essays collected in *Sweet and Sour* and in the columns for *Newsweek, Collier's* and *Newsday*), one shudders in dreadful anticipation of his next blunder. At times he can be exceedingly sharp and funny, but more often he is simultaneously embarrassing and infuriating in his vaingloriousness, vindictiveness, and general bellicosity. For example, in the foreword to *Assembly* he asserts that probably not more than half a dozen people in the world are capable of discerning the techniques he employs in the writing of his short stories! And most of the foreword to *The Cape Cod Lighter* consists of a denunciation of various kinds of critics and of the declaration that most critics are innately hostile to writers because they themselves are frustrated poets, novelists, and dramatists.

O'Hara also contradicts himself. In the preface to his *Five Plays* he avows that his work has rarely been motivated by money, yet in Chapter 13 of *Sweet and Sour* he indicates that that *author*, the real professional, is always interested in money and counts it one measure of his professional achievement. On several occasions he states that the reviewers and their opinions are insignificant, yet he persists in quarreling with them. He declares that he is unconcerned whether or not his work is read by posterity; then he boasts that some of his writing has already survived for a generation and is being read by the children of members of his original audiences. He affects to despise academicians, but he is hurt that he has not received academic prizes and credentials. And then there is that catastrophic statement with which O'Hara began his lead review in the New York *Times Book Review* for September 10, 1950, of Hemingway's *Across the River and Into the Trees:* "The most important author living today, the outstanding author since the death of Shakespeare, has brought out a new novel. The title of the novel is *Across the River and Into the Trees.* The author, of course, is Ernest Hemingway, the most important, the outstanding author out of the millions of writers who have lived since 1616." To paraphrase T. S. Eliot: after such nonsense, what forgiveness?

Fortunately, one does not judge writers' artistic merit by the lack of wisdom, probity, and restraint in their public utterances. However, when one approaches O'Hara's work itself, one remarks similar though less disturbing inconsistencies. O'Hara obviously has keen intelligence, but his ideas are not always followed through to their own inevitable conclusions. To take a crucial case in point, there is considerable ambiguity or irresolution in O'Hara's thinking about the relationship of man and "civilization" or, to use a word more relevant to O'Hara, "society."

As repeatedly demonstrated in this study, O'Hara at his best is much more than a determinist who portrays society as the single overwhelming force shaping man's destiny. However, it would be willful blindness to deny O'Hara's fascination with the interaction between society and the individual. The careers of Julian English, Grace Tate, Gloria Wandrous, and many other O'Hara protagonists demonstrate that human nature and society do often collide. And if we interpret O'Hara rightly, one of his prime conclusions is that society forces upon man duties and roles he cannot fulfill; the result is tension, pain, and rebellion. It also seems obvious that O'Hara, like Dreiser, Hemingway, and Faulkner, is for man and against society. A long passage in *From the Terrace* concludes to this effect: that Christianity, especially the love of one's neighbors, is not inherent in man but a social construct, and that society errs in coercing man to do what is unnatural to him.[1] Many other instances in O'Hara's work lead the reader to infer his belief that society is a cruel, artificial system which causes men endless misery. Writers have built great careers upon shakier theses.

Unfortunately, we remark with equal frequency both explicit and implicit contradictions to the idea that man and society are natural enemies. Underneath the hard-boiled "modern" exterior of much of O'Hara's work, we repeatedly discern a massively solid, traditional, and fundamentally comforting view of society. (Recall Jim Malloy's simultaneous rebelliousness and conservatism?) For example, in *A Rage to Live* are such statements as these: "The world's still one-sided, in favor of the men, because the women like it that way too . . ." and "The nicest people are natural people. Be natural with yourself and other people will recognize that, and be your friends," and "Nobody is as self-sufficient as you think you are . . . sooner or later . . . you need other people."[2] We recall also what O'Hara had written in *Sermons and Soda-Water* about loneliness being the stimulus for love. We bring to mind that, on the eves of their deaths, both Julian English and Gloria Wandrous were about to find their true identities, their places in the common lot. We recollect that Alfred Eaton was exiled because he had failed to make friends. We remember that the worst pain suffered by Robert Millhouser after the murder of his wife was his sense of being cut off from all human communication. We review dozens of instances in the short fiction when life was momentarily illuminated by an act of love or kindness between one human being and another.

Since O'Hara so persistently portrays his people as social animals who need love, communication, and company as much as food and shelter, then *society* can clearly not be wholly an artifice, an invention, a fiendish torture chamber created by an unnamed power; but that society is, in fact, an indispensable condition of human life deriving from human nature itself. Hence, there is ambiguity. But ambiguity in itself need not make all the difference between the great writer and the good one. Part of the difference stems from a further ambiguity—one in O'Hara's emotional response toward man and society; that is, an irresolution in how he *feels* about society. Ambiguity becomes intensified by ambivalence.

To take perhaps the most salient instance, we should consider O'Hara's treatment of the rich. While he has portrayed with wondrous accuracy and vividness what happens in the confrontation between the rich and the poor, and while he has admirably demonstrated that silk coats often cover black hearts and that pure souls are sometimes embodied in tattered and ungainly shapes, we still do not know after twenty-one published volumes precisely how he feels about the rich and the poor and with which he identifies himself. His ambivalence toward the rich is especially tantalizing, at times exasperating, because he is so obviously preoccupied with them. Most consistently, in line with his tacit but fundamental acceptance of society as *given*, O'Hara seems to say: "Here are the rich, I show them to you in all their beauty, power, glory, and frequent iniquity. Here are the poor. I show them to you in all their misery, hardship, want, and frequent nobility. The rich are above. The poor are below. Yes, some of the poor ought to be high and some of the rich ought to be low. But then, that's life. That's the way it is." But *why* is it that way?

To put this major criticism of O'Hara in a phrase, I miss in his works at least one touchstone of greatness: the religious or philosophical dimension, not in the sense of any theology or doctrine, but in the sense of the obsession with ultimates, the quest for fundamental verities—even though those verities sound the everlasting No. O'Hara's special talent has been for the applied, not the theoretical, for the process, not the discovery. He does not ask the most searching questions of all: What are we? How did we get here? Where are we going? What does it all mean?

One also suspects some connection between this refusal or inability to plumb the depths and O'Hara's commitment to the writing of social history. O'Hara as a boy and young man had read John Galsworthy and F. Scott Fitzgerald and had been deeply impressed by them (he wrote of Fitzgerald: "The people were right, the talk was right, the clothes, the cars were real, and the mysticism was a kind of challenge").[3] Later, O'Hara settled upon what he evidently considers his highest calling in the writing of social history, the recording of yesterdays and todays. We find this assertion in the author's preface to *Sermons and Soda Water:*

> I want to get it all down on paper while I can. I am now fifty-five years old and I have lived with as well as in the Twentieth Century from its earliest days. The United States in this Century is what I know, and it is my business to write about it to the best of my ability, with the sometimes special knowledge I have. The Twenties, the Thirties, and the Forties are

already history, but I cannot be content to leave their story in the hands of the historians and the editors of picture books. I want to record the way people talked and thought and felt, and to do it with complete honesty and variety.

There is not the slightest hint of ultimates in this declaration, but there is instead the safer and more comfortable reliance upon the *known*. Nor should we deride the known and O'Hara's attempt to embody it and to dramatize it in the form of fiction, which he has done with high distinction. However, as earlier argued, O'Hara's predilection for social history has often been indulged at severe cost to his achievement as an artist; and, as the present discussion adduces, the greatest art in fiction demands something more than social history.

A final aspect of his work, not yet broached in this study, deserves consideration before an appraisal is made of O'Hara's attainments and distinctions. In *Butterfield 8* this observation appears:

> There comes one time in a man's life, if he is unlucky and leads a full life, when he has a secret so dirty that he knows he will never get rid of it. (Shakespeare knew this and tried to say it, but he said it just as badly as anyone ever said it. "All the perfumes of Arabia" makes you think of all the perfumes of Arabia and nothing more. It is the trouble with all metaphors where human behavior is concerned. People are not ships, chessmen, flowers, race horses, oil paintings, bottles of champagne, excrement, musical instruments, or anything else but people. Metaphors are all right to give you an idea.)[4]

My concern at this point does not involve dirty secrets but O'Hara's attitude toward metaphors. Consistent with his thinking, he employs them rarely; and when he does infrequently bring them into play, as in "Our Friend the Sea" (*The Hat on the Bed*), he is likely to do so self-consciously. While only the most rigid dogmatist of a particular stripe would insist on the fiction writer's use of metaphor, the absence of figurative language in O'Hara's work provides another gauge for measuring the distance between O'Hara and greatness.

As O'Hara's own assertion implies in the passage quoted above, metaphor can be defined as the writer's conception of the connection between *what is* and *what is imagined*; or, to phrase it in another way, the connection between the material and immaterial, the real and sur-real, the physical and the metaphysical. Since O'Hara's work lacks virtually all metaphysical, religious, and spiritual dimension, his refusal to employ metaphor is consistent with his *weltanschauung* but symptomatic of its shortcomings. Thus, he portrays the *real* but too often fails to strike through it to the *Real*. Simply, he omits the Universal, whereas the greatest writers have found metaphor indispensable in their attempt to convey the universal.

Furthermore, the absence of metaphor also signifies a salient defect in O'Hara's style, his use of language. There is too rarely *beauty* in it. One admires his language, rightly so, as a tool which he adapted from his Realistic-Naturalistic predecessors, shaped to his own grasp, and honed to a fine edge to carve out his own kind of slices of life. But great writers are most often innovators of language. They make it anew or they employ it in fresh combinations. After them, language is never the same. Not so with O'Hara. His prose at its best represents craftsmanship of the highest competence, language deployed with intelligence, expertness, authority, and accuracy, but only occasionally does it surpass competence. Even the worst of his novels has its memorable passages and scenes; much of his short fiction represents a technical and linguistic expertise nothing short of remarkable; but the beauty and the splendor of language do not move his reader. Taut, astonishingly clear, suggestive, right, even resonant —his language is all that and more when he is in good form. Yet *it* does not move. Rather, the reader is affected by the probity of the insight, the truth of the portrayal, the vividness with which the writer has visualized his people and situations and breathed them into life.

To take this matter of style one step further, much of what has been said about the limitations in O'Hara's world view and the shortcomings in his handling of ideas would be invalidated if O'Hara were indeed a maker of language, a beautiful writer. In other words, the critic does not consider Hemingway and Faulkner great primarily because they were profound thinkers but because they forged a new language. Their excellence consists less of what they did with their ideas than what they did with their words. Similarly, if O'Hara used words splendidly rather than with competence, albeit the highest competence, we would be compelled to forgive him many of his trespasses. But his prose wields no shining hammer strokes, at least not enough of them, to dazzle us into forgiveness.

Now, to enumerate and review O'Hara's virtues, to be called "highly competent" hardly constitutes disgrace. If the reader of this study has interpreted the foregoing analysis of O'Hara's shortcomings as an injunction to shun the writer's work, he has misconstrued the study's larger intention: to demonstrate why O'Hara is not a great writer, not that he is a poor one. He is, in fact, a very good one. I hesitate to predict that he will join the immortals, but he will certainly be read far beyond his own lifetime and this century, perhaps longer.

Although I can only surmise the extent of his future fame and longevity, I can assert with conviction what he has already accomplished. He has assumed exactly the position in the mid-twentieth century that William Dean Howells and Edith Wharton had in their times. That is, for the past three decades O'Hara has been the foremost interpreter of American manners and, at his best, of American morals as well. Like Howells and Wharton, he has been intensely concerned with the impact of money and class upon character; and his range has often been larger than theirs. Moreover, he has frequently overcome the temptation which seems to inhere to the novelist of manners, to portray only surfaces, and has given penetrating glimpses into the human heart. Not gifted with genius, he has with assiduous application made the most of his large talents and created a *body* of work all the more admirable in a time when more and more talented writers write less and less.

Unlike his near-contemporary Fitzgerald, and others, O'Hara has had the stamina and discipline to trade some of his effort for money, yet continue to work seriously without apparent corruption. His record since 1949 is remarkable: four large and two medium-length novels, five plays, a collection of essays, five *novellas*, and three compendious volumes of short stories—to say nothing of scores of uncollected essays and stories. Furthermore, the great bulk of it manifests the same high competence already noted, dignified by moments of greatness. Quantity in itself deserves small commendation; but, when such quantity conjoins with such high competence, there is cause for praise.

To one who studies the total performance of O'Hara, the critics have been especially unjust to O'Hara in their blindness to the human element in his work. Upon reflection, I find the depiction of O'Hara as cold, disinterested, even cruel, more and more exasperating. Human relationships are the real subject of much of O'Hara's fiction and of all of the best of it. The feelings of parent for child, mate for mate, woman for lover, friend for friend—these and other emotions are O'Hara's real and most profound concern. Nor is he a writer only of man's daylight, waking, rational hours. On occasion he has inquired into the unconscious, the atavistic, the buried life of the mind and heart; and on these occasions he has always provoked the reader into deeper self-knowledge. He has depicted as well as anyone now writing the power of compulsion over man's behavior, just as he has also stirringly depicted the necessity for love and compassion.

Few have written about sexuality more candidly than he. And although he has portrayed men and women in their most intimate actions, he has avoided with unusual success—considering the dangers attendant upon such incendiary subject matter—pandering to the audience's lascivious impulses. Some critics, early and late, who have found O'Hara too strong for their tastes, have even accused him (usually by implication) of being a pornographer. But this charge betrays the accusers' misunderstanding of the nature of pornography and of the salubrious effect of O'Hara's work upon healthy minds. The pornographer always separates his characters' sexual behavior from all other aspects of their conduct and concentrates upon it exclusively. He endows his characters with superhuman erotic ability, and he places them into sexual contact as often and as variously as space permits. Furthermore, their orgiastic sprees never have consequences: all is permitted, and no one either suffers or worries much about it later. Finally, since the pornographer has only one purpose, the excitation of his reader, he structures his erotic scenes so that they build from cold to hot.

One could go on with this analysis, but it seems unnecessary. That anyone could term O'Hara a pornographer—with all of the anguish and aftermath he shows sex to involve, with his careful and detailed portrayal of sexuality as rooted in the whole complex of a character's personality, moral values, social affiliation, life-style—seems the acme of prudish bigotry. O'Hara's deep involvement with his characters' sexual lives (an involvement, by the way, which plays a subordinate part in his short stories) stems not from any dirtymindedness and not from any wish to titillate his readers into buying more of his books, but from his convictions. O'Hara believes that, in order to honestly portray the American man and woman in the twentieth century, one must give sex its due. It has for better or worse a large role in the consciousness of this age, and it would be absurd for any writer who counts himself a Realist to gloss over that fact. Indeed, few of the most esteemed modern writers have done so. In O'Hara's view of man, sex demands recognition as a basic force.[5]

But signs indicate that the long indifference or hostility of many serious critics to O'Hara is changing. The National Book Award for *Ten North Frederick* was the first hopeful indication of an O'Hara reappraisal. Then, in 1964, O'Hara was chosen by the American Academy of Arts and Letters to receive its Award of Merit given every five years for "notable achievement" in the novel. With this award O'Hara joined the distinguished group of previous winners: Theodore Dreiser, Thomas Mann, Ernest Hemingway, and Aldous Huxley. In the award ceremony John Hersey cited O'Hara for his discipline and his vitality, comparing him to Anthony Trollope in his fund of creative energy. The Academy's announcement was even more complimentary, as this quotation indicates:

> Although O'Hara's writings have had enormous popular success they are also highly esteemed by his fellow-writers. His ear for the American language in dialogue is unsurpassed; his prose style is straightforward and unaffected, a splendid implement for the depiction of the small Pennsylvania town whose inhabitants form a large part of his fictional world. His main interest is in people, and he writes about them with the insights drawn from long acquaintance with their lives and status, their aspirations and frustrations. Like all major novelists, he has a tragic view of mankind, but it is not a narrow view, nor does it preclude wild flights of humor and the most minute observations of character and behavior.
>
> As the years have passed O'Hara's craftsmanship has grown more and more masterly, while his creative output seems inexhaustible, an achievement rarely paralleled in American literature.[6]

This summary is accurate and thorough. Few writers would be ashamed to have it inscribed as their epitaph, but it is to be hoped that O'Hara still has many years of productive effort remaining to him.

As suggested by Hersey's comparison of O'Hara to Trollope, there are strong traditions and large bodies of fine work within which he might be placed. One discerns resemblances to Balzac, Chekhov, Galsworthy, but these need not be labored. As to his rank among his colleagues and in his own century, I can be somewhat more precise. In the American fiction of this age Hemingway and Faulkner unquestionably occupy a place apart —in the first rank. O'Hara is somewhere in the upper half of the second rank at whose head we would find Dreiser, Lewis, Fitzgerald, and Wolfe. While O'Hara has not written any single work of the quality of *The Grapes of Wrath,* he deserves equal stature with Steinbeck; and, if one compares their relative performances of the past fifteen years, O'Hara is the better. Furthermore, although he will probably not attain the kind of special historic niche belonging to Sherwood Anderson and to John Dos Passos, the whole body of O'Hara's work has merit comparable to theirs. He is a far more consistent and serious writer than Lardner, and in the main superior to Robert Penn Warren, James Gould Cozzens, or John P. Marquand.

This sort of ordering and categorization is extremely hazardous to all concerned and it must be understood that I wish not to establish a new kingdom for O'Hara, but simply to claim a modest plot of ground whereupon this deserving and hitherto homeless author might be settled. Perhaps it would be best after all to let O'Hara speak for himself. Asked by an interviewer to assume for the moment the guise of literary critic and so sum up the career of John O'Hara, O'Hara said: "Better than anyone else he told the truth about his time, the first half of the twentieth century. He was a professional. He wrote honestly and well."[7]

This seems a reasonable and fair assessment. Why not let it stand?

Notes and References

Chapter One

1. I have computed this from the *PMLA* Annual Bibliography, published in the May issue each year, after consulting the issues for 1961-1964.

2. Arthur Hobson Quinn, *et al.*, eds., *The Literature of the American People* (New York, 1951). Robert E. Spiller, *et al.*, eds., *Literary History of the United States* (New York, 1953). In this edition O'Hara is mentioned on pages 1314 and 1398. In the recently revised edition of this work (1963), the coverage of O'Hara has been expanded to two paragraphs. Even so, he is considered less significant than James Gould Cozzens.

3. Max J. Herzberg, ed., *The Reader's Encyclopedia of American Literature* (New York, 1962), p. 826.

4. For influential early estimates of O'Hara see John Peale Bishop, "The Missing All," *Virginia Quarterly Review*, XIII (Jan., 1937), 120-21; and Edmund Wilson, "The Boys in the Back Room: James M. Cain and John O'Hara," *New Republic*, CIII (November 11, 1940), 665-66. The judgment of O'Hara in the *Literary History of the United States* is virtually a synthesis of these two views.

5. Albert Van Nostrand, *The Denatured Novel* (Indianapolis, 1960), pp. 211-14.

6. John W. Aldridge, "Highbrow Authors and Middlebrow Books," *Playboy*, XI (April, 1964), 166-74.

7. Cf. John Portz, "John O'Hara up to Now," *College English*, XVI (May, 1955), 493-99, 516; E. Russell Carson, *The Fiction of John O'Hara* (Pittsburgh, 1961); and Jesse Bier, "O'Hara's *Appointment in Samarra*: His First and Only Real Novel," *College English*, XXV (November, 1963), 135-41. The subtitle of Mr. Bier's essay denotes a prevailing academic attitude.

Chapter Two

1. According to Walter S. Farquhar, O'Hara's friend and guide during his stay on the Pottsville *Journal*, O'Hara was not dismissed from the paper but "farmed out." This information was conveyed by Mr. Farquhar in an interview with the present writer, Pottsville, Pennsylvania, April 1, 1964. For O'Hara's fond reminiscences of his summer visits with his grandparents, see *Sweet and Sour* (New York, 1954), pp. 113-15.

2. Walter S. Farquhar, "Editorial Musings," Pottsville *Republican*, June 3, 1958.

3. In "Appointment with O'Hara," *Collier's*, CXXXV (April 29, 1955), O'Hara described the house he lived in as a boy with nostalgia and affection.

4. Samuel T. Wiley, *Biographical and Portrait Cyclopedia of Schuylkill County, Pennsylvania;* revised and edited by Henry W. Ruoff (Philadelphia, 1893).

5. John O'Hara, quoted in Farquhar, "Editorial Musings," Pottsville *Republican*, March 21, 1950. In a subsequent column, March 28, 1950, Farquhar corrects O'Hara's account and adds further detail, all of it complimentary to Dr. O'Hara. The train-wreck episode probably was the basis for an episode in O'Hara's *novella, A Family Party* (1956).

6. Farquhar, interview.

7. D. W. Davis, Curator, Schuylkill County Historical Society, in an interview with the present author, Pottsville, April 2, 1964.

8. Farquhar and Davis, interviews. Also, Miss Edith Patterson, interview with the author, Pottsville, April 2, 1964. Miss Patterson was formerly head librarian at the Pottsville Free Library; she and Mrs. O'Hara once belonged to the same French club. Another Pottsville lady, who wishes not to be identified, has said, obviously disturbed by the content of some of O'Hara's books, "John seems to be a different branch of the family. He's nothing like the O'Haras I know. Mart [a younger brother, still resident in Pottsville] is so quiet. I also knew his mother and sister, and they were very refined."

9. Beverly Gary, "John O'Hara," part II, New York *Post* (May 19, 1959), p. 78.

10. John O'Hara, "Appointment with O'Hara," *Collier's*, CXXXIII (Feb. 5, 1954).

11. John O'Hara, " 'Don't Say It Never Happened,' " New York *Herald Tribune Books* (April 8, 1962), p. 3. Farquhar, "Editorial Musings," Pottsville *Republican*, June 16, 1959, remembers O'Hara riding his horse up and down the sidelines during football practice at Pottsville High School. In "From Winter Quarters," *Circus* [Ringling Brothers Summer Circus Program], Summer, 1961, pp. 8, 60, O'Hara recalls how as a boy he greeted the arrival of the circus in town by riding his Shetland pony and wearing his cowboy outfit, hoping Pottsvillians would mistake him for a member of the show.

12. O'Hara alludes to the jail episode, but without further detail, in "Appointment with O'Hara," *Collier's*, CXXXIV (August 6, 1954). The account of the attack on the German-American club appears in his *Newsweek* column, "Entertainment Week," XIX (January 26, 1942), 64. Also see *Collier's* August 8, 1955, for O'Hara's amusing

confession that in 1919, while his father was away as a spectator at the Dempsey-Willard fight, he sneaked Dr. O'Hara's car out of the garage to take some of his friends for a ride. During the excursion, however, a radial rod snapped. Dr. O'Hara's wrath, upon his return, was considerable.

13. Both "The Doctor's Son" and "It Must Have Been Spring," are contained in *The Doctor's Son and Other Stories* (New York, 1935). The quotation is taken from page 54. The influenza epidemic recounted in the first story has a wholly factual basis in the epidemic of 1918-19. Pottsvillians still remember it with horror. In reference to O'Hara's direct experience of the epidemic as his father's driver, as narrated in "The Doctor's Son," Miss Patterson states, "There is this to be said for John. He met life head-on at a time when other boys would have been sheltered."

14. John O'Hara, "There Is Nothing Like a Norfolk," *Holiday*, XIV (September, 1953), 14. In his *Collier's* column for December 23, 1955, O'Hara sketches the exploits of a group of young roisterers, himself prominently included, who called themselves "The Purity League." During the Christmas holiday the League declared its attitude toward the town's more righteous gentry by placing recently emptied whiskey bottles on the front porches of its critics.

15. Beverly Gary, New York *Post*, May 19, 1959.

16. "John O'Hara at 58: A Rage to Write," *Newsweek*, LXI (June 3, 1963), 56. Between prep schools O'Hara had already worked briefly at a number of jobs. In the year after his graduation from Niagara, he began at the Pottsville *Journal*.

17. Beverly Gary, *op. cit.*

18. Beverly Gary identifies the girl as Margaretta Archibald. Corroborative sources, although they do not name the young lady, are Farquhar and Miss Patterson.

19. *Butterfield 8* (New York, 1935), p. 68.

20. Miss Patterson is the main source for the analysis of anti-Irish sentiment among Pottsville's upper class. For an illuminating account of the Molly Maguires see William V. Shannon, *The American Irish* (New York, 1963). Shannon's book also contains a provocative interpretation of O'Hara's career.

21. *Assembly* (New York, 1961), pp. 229-30.

22. O'Hara told Harvey Breit, in a 1949 interview: "The newspaper influence is good for the writer. It teaches economy of words. It makes you write faster. When you're on rewrite as I was, you can't fool around at half-past nine trying to write beautiful lacy prose." Cf. Harvey Breit, *The Writer Observed* (New York, 1961), p. 60. Of O'Hara's newspaper work in Pottsville, Farquhar told me during an interview: "John liked to write but he didn't like to report. He didn't

have the news sense. He was too impatient to do routine drudgery, too much of an artist. He missed routine assignments because he didn't think they were worth covering."

23. Quoted in Farquhar, "Editorial Musings," Pottsville *Republican*, March 21, 1950.

24. Beverly Gary, *op. cit.*, and John O'Hara, " 'Don't Say It Never Happened,' " *op. cit.*

25. The Hemingway anecdote appeared in O'Hara's "Entertainment Week," *Newsweek*, XIX (February 9, 1942), 63.

26. Jack Keating, "John O'Hara's World of Yale, Society, and Sex," *Cosmopolitan*, CXLIX (September, 1960), 61.

27. "Editorial Musings," Pottsville *Journal*, March 27, 1945. In a later column, June 3, 1958, Farquhar theorized that O'Hara's "clinical knowledge" of people and his "clinical urge" to probe beneath the surface of life may have been inspired by his doctor-father. It is a challenging surmise.

28. *Newsweek* (June 3, 1963), 56.

29. *We're Friends Again, Sermons and Soda Water*, III (New York, 1960), p. 54. Soon after this statement Malloy avows that, while he would never convert from Catholicism to another religion, he will never again be a practicing Catholic. From all appearances, Malloy speaks for John O'Hara.

30. *Assembly*, p. 229.

31. *Imagine Kissing Pete, Sermons and Soda Water*, II, pp. 71-72.

Chapter Three

1. Quoted in Lewis Nichols, "Talk with John O'Hara," New York *Times Book Review* (November 27, 1955), p. 16.

2. John O'Hara, *Appointment in Samarra* (New York, 1934), p. 266. All subsequent quotations from the novel are noted in the text of the discussion.

3. Albert William Levi, *Literature, Philosophy, and the Imagination* (Bloomington, Indiana: 1962), p. 264.

4. Arthur Mizener, "Afterword," *Appointment in Samarra* (New York, 1963), p. 208.

5. Clinically, Julian's behavior fits into one of the classic patterns of sado-masochism: his aggressions towards others stems from his need to invite punishment, while the almost sexual nature of his feelings when he knows punishment is forthcoming is both a re-enactment of the child's relationship with the father and a clue to his own arrested emotional development.

6. I borrow these descriptive terms in my discussion of point of view from Norman Friedman's seminal article, "Point of View in Fic-

tion: The Development of a Critical Concept," *PMLA*, LXX (December, 1955), 1160-84. Friedman's article has also been reprinted in a number of collections.

7. Quoted in Breit, *The Writer Observed, op. cit.*, p. 59.

8. John O'Hara, *A Rage to Live* (New York, 1949), p. 499. All subsequent references are included in the discussion itself.

9. Concluding couplet of O'Hara's quotation from Alexander Pope's "Epistle to a Lady," several lines of which serve as the novel's epigraph.

10. See O'Hara's remarks regarding his portrayal of Grace and defending his treatment of his characters' sex lives, quoted in Jack Keating, "John O'Hara's World of Yale, Society, and Sex," *Cosmopolitan*, CXLIX (September, 1960), 60.

11. John O'Hara, *From the Terrace* (New York, 1958), p. 502. All subsequent references appear in the text.

12. In conversation with the present writer, Lexington, Kentucky, winter, 1955.

13. John O'Hara, *Ten North Frederick* (New York, 1955), p. 408. Other quotations from this source are identified in the discussion.

14. "Novel by O'Hara Wins Book Prize," New York *Times* (February 8, 1956), p. 24. The National Book Awards, given each year since 1950 for fiction, non-fiction, and poetry, are now undoubtedly more prestigious than the Pulitzer awards in American literary circles because they need not conform to any conditions other than literary merit. The judges who selected O'Hara's work for recognition were Carlos Baker, John Brooks, Granville Hicks, Saunders Redding, and Mark Schorer. Among the winners of the National Book Award have been Nelson Algren, William Faulkner, Saul Bellow, Wright Morris, John Cheever, and Philip Roth.

15. John O'Hara, *Sweet and Sour* (New York, 1954), pp. 154, 84. See also "Appointment with O'Hara," *Colliers,* CXXXIII (April 16, 1954), in which O'Hara wrote: "I'm on a first-name basis with two authentic Vanderbilts, two genuine Whitneys, and one former Astor, which is darn' good for a boy from Pottsville, Pennsylvania. By and large, I think the experience has been good for all of us: the snobbish poor, the democratic rich."

16. "Lyons" is O'Hara's fictional projection of the actual town of Lykens, where he spent summers with his maternal grandparents. We also note a number of similarities between the author's boyhood and that of his narrator, Gerald Higgins.

17. John O'Hara, *Ourselves to Know* (New York, 1960), pp. 47-48. All subsequent references noted in the discussion.

18. This is but one of several grave blunders committed by Mr. Vidal in his essay-review "Appointment with O'Hara," *New York*

Review of Books, II (April 16, 1964), 5-7. The source of the critic's error in accepting Elizabeth's portrayal without further question can be located in Vidal's conviction that O'Hara is "never anything but dead-serious." That is, Vidal finds O'Hara's work totally lacking in wit, humor, irony, and in a sense of his characters' follies.

19. John O'Hara, *Elizabeth Appleton* (New York, 1963), p. 83. All further quotations identified in the text.

20. John O'Hara, *A Family Party* (New York, 1956), pp. 41-42, 35.

Chapter Four

1. John O'Hara, *Butterfield 8* (New York, 1935), pp. 305, 306. Most subsequent references are included in the discussion.

2. This biographical data is drawn from several sources, as follows: Maxine Block, ed., *Current Biography* (New York, H. W. Wilson Company, 1941), pp. 633-35; Beverly Gary, "John O'Hara," New York *Post*, May 18, 1959, p. 22 and May 20, 1959, p. 50; Wolcott Gibbs, "Watch Out for Mr. O'Hara," *Saturday Review of Literature*, XVII (February 19, 1938), 10-12; John K. Hutchens, "John O'Hara From Pottsville, Pa.," New York *Herald Tribune Books*, December 4, 1955, p. 2; Jack Keating, "John O'Hara's World of Yale, Society, and Sex," *Cosmopolitan*, CXLIX (September, 1960), 59-63; Stanley J. Kunitz and Howard Haycraft, *Twentieth Century Authors* (New York, 1942), pp. 1044-45; "John O'Hara at 58: A Rage to Write," *Newsweek*, LXI (June 3, 1963), 53-58; and Robert Van Gelder, *Writers and Writing* (New York, 1946), pp. 59-61.

3. Van Gelder, p. 60.

4. Cf. John O'Hara, "Appointment with O'Hara," *Collier's*, CXXXIV (October 29, 1954), and CXXXVI (September 30, 1955). In his foreword to his volume of collected plays, O'Hara named his writing for Hollywood as one of three kinds he had done primarily for money, the others being journalism and some of his early work for the *New Yorker*. Over the years O'Hara worked for four major studios: Paramount, Metro-Goldwyn-Mayer, RKO-Radio, and 20th Century Fox, mainly as a "polish guy," *i.e.*, revising scripts originally prepared by others. According to Gary, New York *Post*, May 21, 1959, p. 24, O'Hara's efforts as a screen writer were less esteemed than his fiction. However, among the benefits derived from his Hollywood career were a number of close friendships, including those with Robert Benchley and F. Scott Fitzgerald. See O'Hara's moving essay on Fitzgerald, "In Memory of F. Scott Fitzgerald," *New Republic*, CIX (March 3, 1941), 311.

5. The New York *Times*, the primary source for my resumé of the Starr Faithfull case, carried daily stories about it for almost a month beginning June 9, 1931. By late July the episode had ceased to merit

front-page interest although it had occasional notice as late as December.

6. *Butterfield 8,* pp. 188 ff.

7. John O'Hara, *Hope of Heaven* (New York, 1938), p. 18. This self-portrayal as a leftist sympathizer must be set against O'Hara's association with the rich and the growing political conservatism characteristic of him during the past fifteen years. See, for example, O'Hara's remarks on the Goldwater-Johnson presidential campaign, as published in his weekly columns for *Newsday* during the fall of 1964.

8. John O'Hara, *Hellbox* (New York, 1947), pp. 165-66. Future references included in the text.

9. The quotations in the order of their appearance are from *We're Friends Again, Sermons and Soda Water* (New York, 1960), pp. 60, 109-10.

10. Like most of O'Hara's short stories, the individual Pal Joey tales first appeared in the *New Yorker* and were later collected for book publication: *Pal Joey* (New York, 1940).

11. John O'Hara, *Files on Parade* (New York, 1939), p. 78.

12. John O'Hara, *Assembly* (New York, 1961), p. 144.

13. John O'Hara, *Five Plays* (New York, 1961), p. xiii. Subsequent references in the text.

14. Cf. John O'Hara, *Pal Joey: The Libretto and Lyrics.* Lyrics by Lorenz Hart. Music by Richard Rodgers. (New York, 1952). Although the stage adaptation of *Pal Joey* has some historical significance as one of the first carefully plotted musical plays, no doubt much of its success can be attributed to the music, cast, and production. The score includes two songs which are now "standards": "Bewitched, Bothered, and Bewildered," and "I Could Write A Book." Moreover, the original cast featured Gene Kelly, Vivienne Segal, and June Havoc. The revival won both the New York Drama Critics' and the Donaldson Awards as the best musical of 1952.

15. In his initial "Appointment with O'Hara" column for *Collier's,* CXXXIII (February 5, 1954) O'Hara wrote: "Through the years I have met literally thousands of actors and actresses, playwrights, directors, singers, composers, lyric writers, press agents, box-office people, managers, cameramen, circus people, agents, angels, musicians —and husbands, wives, and mothers of the aforesaid. Most of them I am pleased to call my friends; some of them I don't like, and of course there are other thousands I don't know." However, against this statement, one must measure the persistently hostile depiction O'Hara gives his entertainment-world characters in his fiction. The same *Collier's* essay has other data concerning O'Hara's Hollywood career.

16. John O'Hara, *The Big Laugh* (New York, 1962), pp. 94-95. Further references included in the text.

Chapter Five

1. In his foreword to the Modern Library edition of *Appointment in Samarra* (New York, 1953), O'Hara named Fitzgerald, Sinclair Lewis, Galsworthy, Booth Tarkington, and Owen Johnson—especially Fitzgerald and Lewis—as writers who had influenced him. Although he denied any conscious borrowing from Hemingway, he acknowledged that Hemingway's example had probably been instructive to him in conceiving the form of his short stories. O'Hara also said that, for his stories, he had learned a good deal from Dorothy Parker about the handling of point-of-view and from Ring Lardner about the writing of realistic dialogue.

2. What has been said about the sensibility story also largely applies to the so-called "*New Yorker* story." It should be noted that O'Hara was one of those who originated the *New Yorker* story and developed it to a high degree of sophistication. Incidentally, the term "sensibility story" refers to the degree of awareness and sensitivity to the nuances of human behavior necessary to both the writer and reader. It also applies to this kind of story's prime concern: the sensibilities of its characters. Latterly, the term has sometimes been used pejoratively to indicate the febrility and thinness characteristic of such stories as published in the literary quarterlies.

3. *Files on Parade,* p. 37.

4. My reference for the labels employed in naming the various points of view is once again Norman Friedman, "Point of View in Fiction," cited in Chapter Three above. The terms "dramatic" (or "scenic") and "panoramic" come, of course, from Percy Lubbock's well-known *The Craft of Fiction.*

5. *The Doctor's Son and Other Stories,* p. 81.

6. *Ibid.,* p. 276.

7. *Hellbox,* pp. 30-31.

8. *Pipe Night,* pp. 64-65.

9. *Ibid.,* p. 67.

10. While other analogues could undoubtedly be cited by those familiar with the corpus of Chekhov's short fiction, "Radio" reminds me most of Chekhov's "The Lottery Ticket," a story sometimes anthologized.

11. We can also surmise that O'Hara's break with the *New Yorker* was partly responsible for his abstention from the short story form. This rupture in the long-standing association between O'Hara and the magazine which had published most of his stories came about as the result of a slashing review by Brendan Gill of *A Rage to Live* in the *New Yorker,* XXV (August 20, 1949), 64-65. O'Hara was deeply aggrieved, not without reason, at what he considered the disloyalty of

the magazine in printing so savage an attack upon one of its most important contributors. He therefore resolved not to publish any further stories in the *New Yorker* until suitable reparation was made. The rift endured for eleven years but was apparently settled to O'Hara's satisfaction.

12. One can only speculate that the death of his wife and his own grave illness were responsible for the more serious tone of O'Hara's later work. Certainly the illness, by O'Hara's own admission, necessitated a great change in his habits. His health no longer permitting his full participation in the gay night life of New York café society, O'Hara settled down to the slower pace of Princeton, New Jersey, and became engaged in that tremendous surge of literary productivity which has produced a book a year for the past ten years. The beginnings of this change can probably be discerned in 1945, with the death of O'Hara's dear friend Robert Benchley. As O'Hara put it, when Benchley died "the party was over." Cf. *Newsweek*, LXI (June 3, 1963), 57.

13. *Assembly*, p. 63.

14. *Ibid.*, p. 270.

Chapter Six

1. *From the Terrace*, pp. 808-10. The passage is so long and so dispersed that it forbids direct quotation. It is one of the rare instances in O'Hara's work which directly presents his world view. In this instance he speaks through Alfred Eaton.

2. *A Rage to Live*, pp. 346, 488, 279.

3. John O'Hara, "In Memory of F. Scott Fitzgerald," *New Republic*, CIV (March 3, 1941), 311.

4. *Butterfield 8*, p. 298.

5. Of all the charges which the critics have levied against O'Hara during the years, perhaps none has wounded him more than the accusation that he is a writer of dirty books. He has replied to it on a number of occasions. For example, in 1960 he told an interviewer:

Of course, I write about sex. . . . It's the Life Force . . . But no one can accuse me of writing smut and make the accusation stick. . . . You can drag sex in by the heels and sell it to a kind of slobbering trade, but your book won't outlast its brief span of notoriety. Take Joyce or D. H. Lawrence; if their books had nothing beyond the sexy passages that outraged the bluenoses, they would long since have been forgotten. Then you get the kind of writer who shies away from sex. For example, the late John Marquand kept coming up to it, sex, and refusing to treat it. If sex has an important place in my books, it's because it has an important place in life.

Quoted in Keating, "John O'Hara's World of Yale, Society, and Sex," *op. cit.*, 60. He also wrote in his *Collier's* "Appointment with O'Hara" column for March 2, 1956:

> I would like here to make a statement that I have often made in private. I have lived an extremely full life, experiencing exquisite pleasure and all but unbearable sorrow and pain; loving some, hating a few, pitying many, and scorning the contemptible; joyful of my accomplishments and stung by my failures. Throughout it all I have been pleased by the circumstance that has enabled me to earn my living at the job I love best, which is writing. I am a simple, worldly-wise man and practically nothing except stupid cruelty can shock me, and I have never written a word for the purpose of shocking anyone else. But I have often been disgusted by people who take pleasure in scatological humor, in the telling and the listening, and yet are genuinely or otherwise offended by any and all reference to the function called sex.

6. The Academy's announcement of its Award of Merit was reproduced as a full-page advertisement (taken by O'Hara's publisher, Random House) in the New York *Times Book Review,* May 24, 1964), p. 9. Mr. Hersey's presentation speech was communicated to me in a letter from Felicia Giffen, Assistant to the President of the Academy. Although the names of the judges for the award are kept confidential, they are all members of the Department of Literature of the National Institute of Arts and Letters. Quite by accident I learned of the identities of two. They are internationally renowned scholar-critics who teach at two of our most distinguished universities. That O'Hara should have won the support of such men is indeed encouraging, and perhaps prophetic.

7. Quoted in Miles A. Smith, "O'Hara Walks a Lot, Writes a Lot," Associated Press, release for December 31, 1961.

Selected Bibliography

PRIMARY SOURCES

1. Novels and Novellas

Appointment in Samarra. New York: Harcourt, Brace, 1934.
Butterfield 8. New York: Harcourt, Brace, 1935.
Hope of Heaven. New York: Harcourt, Brace, 1938.
A Rage to Live. New York: Random House, 1949.
The Farmer's Hotel. New York: Random House, 1951.
Ten North Frederick. New York: Random House, 1955.
A Family Party. New York: Random House, 1956.
From the Terrace. New York: Random House, 1958.
Ourselves to Know. New York: Random House, 1960.
Sermons and Soda Water: A Trilogy. New York: Random House, 1960.
The Big Laugh. New York: Random House, 1962.
Elizabeth Appleton. New York: Random House, 1963.

2. Short Stories and Collections

The Doctor's Son and Other Stories. New York: Harcourt, Brace, 1935.
Files on Parade. New York: Harcourt, Brace, 1939.
Pal Joey. New York: Harcourt, Brace, 1940.
Pipe Night. New York: Duell, Sloan and Pearce, 1945.
Here's O'Hara. New York: Duell, Sloan and Pearce, 1946.
Hellbox. New York: Random House, 1947.
Selected Short Stories. New York: Modern Library (Random House), 1957.
Assembly. New York: Random House, 1961.
The Cape Cod Lighter. New York: Random House, 1962.
49 Stories. New York: Modern Library (Random House), 1963. (Consists of the stories in *Assembly* and *The Cape Cod Lighter*.)
The Hat on the Bed. New York: Random House, 1964.
The Horse Knows the Way. New York: Random House, 1964.

3. Plays

Pal Joey: The Libretto and Lyrics. New York: Random House, 1952.
Five Plays. New York: Random House, 1961.

4. Essays

Sweet and Sour. New York: Random House, 1954.
Three Views of the Novel. With Irving Stone and MacKinlay Kantor. Washington: Reference Department, the Library of Congress, 1957. (Pamphlet)

5. *Uncollected Writings*
 (*not* including occasional pieces in daily newspapers)

A. *Essays*

"Football: Four Downs and a Fumble," *New Yorker*, IX (November 1933) 45-46.

"Football: Princeton Visits the Bowl," *New Yorker*, IX (December 9, 1933) 85-87.

"Take It!" *New Republic*, CI (December 27, 1939), 287.

"In Memory of F. Scott Fitzgerald," *New Republic*, CIV (March 3, 1941), 311.

"Entertainment Week," weekly column in *Newsweek*, volumes XVI-XIX, July 15, 1940, through February 16, 1942.

"Nothing From Joe?" *Liberty*, XXI (December 9, 1944), 20-21.

"The New Expense Account Society," *Flair*, I (May, 1950), 22-23, 110-11.

"Some Authors of 1951 Speaking for Themselves: John O'Hara," New York *Herald Tribune Books*, October 7, 1951, p. 6.

"There Is Nothing Like A Norfolk," *Holiday*, XIV (September, 1953), 14, 17.

"Appointment with O'Hara," bi-weekly column in *Collier's*, CXXXIII-CXXXVIII, February 5, 1954, through September 28, 1956.

"Don't Say It Never Happened," New York *Herald Tribune Books*, April 8, 1962, p. 3.

"My Turn," weekly column in *Newsday*, beginning October 3, 1964.

"The Wayward Reader," *Holiday*, XXXVI (December, 1964), 31-34.

"Memoirs of a Sentimental Duffer," *Holiday*, XXXVII (May, 1965), 66-67.

B. *Stories and Sketches:* published in the *New Yorker* unless otherwise noted.

1928 (vol. IV)

"The Alumnae Bulletin" (May 5), 101.

"Tennis" (June 9), 85.

"Did You Know?" (July 14), 41.

"Spring 3100" (Sept. 8), 56.

"A Safe and Sane Fourth" (Sept. 15), 79-82.

"The Halloween Party" (Sept. 22), 81-85.

"Taking Up Sport" (Oct. 13), 58, 63.

"The Coal Fields" (Oct. 20), 85-88.

"The Boss' Present" (Dec. 1), 56, 58, 62.

"The Yule in Retrospect" (Dec. 29), 40-41.

1929 (vol. V)

"Theatre" (Jan. 5), 70.

"Fifty-cent Meal" (Jan. 12), 63.

"House Organ" (March 23), 113.
"Fifteen Minutes for Efficiency" (March 30), 47.
"New Apparatus" (April 6), 61.
"Appreciation" (April 13), 97.
"Mr. Bonner" (May 25), 74.
"Fun for the Kiddies," (June 1), 76.
"The Tournament" (June 8), 81.
"Convention" (June 15), 80.
"Holes in Stockings" (June 22), 52.
"Conditions at the Pool" (July 5), 45.
"Mr. Rosenthal," (July 20), 24.
"The Boss Talks" (Aug. 3), 43.
"Unconditioned Reflexes" (Aug. 31), 58.
"Staff Picture" (Sept. 7), 84.
"Mauve Starts Early Grid Drill" (Sept. 21), 101.
"Out of the West" (Sept. 28), 51.
"Between the Halves" (Oct. 12), 85.
"The Cannons Are a Disgrace" (Oct. 19), 105.
"Halloween Party" (Oct. 26), 36.
"Getting Ready for 1930" (Nov. 9), 77.
"Americanization" (Nov. 23), 81.
"Merrie, Merrie, Merrie" (Dec. 7), 100.
"Memo and Another Memo" (Dec. 14), 89.

1930 (vol. VI)
"Beaux Arts" (Jan. 25), 30.
"Suits Pressed" (Feb. 8), 28.
"Mr. Cleary Misses a Party" (Feb. 22), 49.
"Delphian Hits Girl's Cage-Game Foes" (March 8), 92.
"The Elevator Starter" (March 15), 80.
"Conversation with a Russian" (March 29), 43.
"Little Rememberances" (April 12), 108.
"A Convert to Equitation" (May 3), 97.
"Don't Let It Get You" (May 10), 51.
"The New Office" (May 17), 112.
"Most Likely to Succeed" (June 7).
"Paper Drinking Cups" (July 26), 47, 49.
"Old Boy" (Oct. 18), 28.
"Varsity Manager" (Oct. 25), 87-88.
"Portrait of a Referee" (Nov. 15), 80-82.
"John" (Dec. 27), 28.

1931 (vol. VII)
"Getting a Drink" (Jan. 10), 60-61.
"One Reason for Betsy's Diffidence" (Feb. 28), 65.
"Divorce" (April 11), 69-71.

"The Office Switchboard" (April 25), 71-72.
"Revolt Among the Women" (May 9), 73.
"Papa and Smoking" (May 16), 68-69.
"Ninety Cents for a Sardine" (May 23), 75.
"Help the Younger Element" (June 6), 75.
"Holiday Plans" (June 27), 46-48.
"Nancy and Mr. Zinzindorf" (Sept. 26), 65.
"Paolo and Francesca" (Oct. 24), 56-57.
"Let Us Hang on to It" (Nov. 7), 56-57.
". . . His Partner, Henry T. Collins" (Nov. 28), 76-78.

1932 (vol. VIII)
"Good Evening, Ladies and Gentlemen . . ." (April 30), 19-20.
"It Is Easy Enough to Blame Russia" (Aug. 13), 34-36.

1933 (vol. IX)
"You Need A Rest" (Jan. 14), 57-58.
"If I Was Brought Up a Holy Roller" (Sept. 16), 54-55.
"My Friend in Washington" (Sept. 23), 20.

1935
"Stand-Up," *Colliers,* XCVI (Nov. 30), 17.

1936
"Pretty Little Mrs. Harper," *Scribner's Magazine,* C (Aug.), 92-93.

1944
"Conversation at Lunch," *Good Housekeeping,* CXIX (July), 28.
"Name in the Book," *Good Housekeeping,* CXIX (Dec.), 38, 172-73.

1946 (vol. XXII)
"Pilgrimage" (Nov. 9), 27-30.
"One for the Road" (Nov. 30), 37-38.

1947 (vol. XXIII)
"Not Always" (Jan. 11), 23-24.
"The Lady Takes an Interest" (June 28), 22-23.
"Interior with Figures" (July 19), 22-23.
"The Last of Haley" (Aug. 30), 21-23.
"The Heart of Lee W. Lee" (Sept. 13), 31-33.
"The Dry Murders" (Oct. 18), 33-34.
"Eileen" (Dec. 20), 25-26.

1948 (vol. XXIV)
"Nil Nisi" (Jan. 10), 23-25.
"Requiescat" (April 3), 27-30.

1949 (vol. XXV)
"The Frozen Face" (April 23), 22-24.
"The Industry and the Professor" (July 16), 16-20.
"Grief" (Oct. 22), 28-29.
"The Kids" (Nov. 26), 32-34.

1959
"That First Husband," *Saturday Evening Post*, CCXXXII (Nov. 21), 23-24, 52.

1962
"Trip to Sea," *Blackwood's Magazine*, CCXCII (Oct.), 338-52.

1964 (vol. XL)
"Christmas Poem" (Dec. 19), 34-39.

1965 (vol. XLI)
"The Gambler" (May 1), 40-42.
"Neighborhood" (May 15), 49-53.

SECONDARY SOURCES

1. *Books*

BREIT, HARVEY. *The Writer Observed* (1956). New York: Collier Books, 1961. Early section attacks O'Hara's writings as a columnist and journalist; later pages transcribe an interview with O'Hara.

BROWN, JOHN MASON. *As They Appear*. New York: McGraw-Hill, 1962. Favorable review of the revival of O'Hara's musical play *Pal Joey*.

CARSON, E. RUSSELL. *The Fiction of John O'Hara*. Pittsburgh: University of Pittsburgh Press, 1961; 73 pp. The only extensive critical treatment of O'Hara to date. Contains some provocative insights into O'Hara as novelist of manners, but marred by incompleteness, poor documentation, and clumsy writing.

FADIMAN, CLIFTON. *Party of One*. Cleveland and New York: World, 1955. Three generally hostile reviews of *Appointment in Samarra*, *Butterfield 8*, and *Hope of Heaven*.

GURKO, LEO. *The Angry Decade*. New York: Dodd, Mead, 1947. Views *Appointment in Samarra* and O'Hara's earlier short stories as echoes of the Depression era.

HUTCHENS, JOHN K. Foreword to John O'Hara's *49 Stories*. New York: Random House, 1963. A persuasive summary of O'Hara's virtues by one of his few consistent supporters.

KAZIN, ALFRED. *On Native Grounds* (1942). Garden City: Anchor Books, 1956. Discusses O'Hara as a Naturalist, but finds his work superficial.

―――――. *Contemporaries*. Boston: Little, Brown, 1962. Interprets *From the Terrace* as a debasement of the American writers' ambition to create the "Great American Novel."

LEVI, ALBERT WILLIAM. *Literature, Philosophy, and the Imagination*. Bloomington: Indiana University Press, 1962. Argues that *Appointment in Samarra* illustrates one modern concept of fate in which the novelist portrays tragedy as resulting from social pressure.

MIZENER, ARTHUR. Afterword. John O'Hara's *Appointment in Samarra*. New York: New American Library, 1963. Perhaps the most cogent statement of the prevailing belief that O'Hara best succeeds as a social commentator.

PRESCOTT, ORVILLE. *In My Opinion*. Indianapolis: Bobbs-Merrill, 1952. Slashing attack upon O'Hara which concludes that his work is marred by cynicism and an overemphasis of sex.

SHANNON, WILLIAM V. *The American Irish*. New York: Macmillan, 1963. Treats O'Hara's work as the expression both of its author's Irish background and his attempt to escape from it. Provocative.

VAN DOREN, MARK. *The Great Ideas Today*. Chicago: Encyclopedia Britannica, 1961. Concludes that O'Hara depends too heavily upon money, liquor, and sex for his character motivations, but also recognizes O'Hara's talent.

VAN GELDER, ROBERT. *Writers and Writing*. New York: Scribners, 1946. Largely the transcript of an interview with O'Hara in which the writer recollects how he composed *Appointment in Samarra*.

VAN NOSTRAND, ALBERT. *The Denatured Novel*. Indianapolis: Bobbs-Merrill, 1960. Establishes O'Hara as one of the imitators of the Hemingway method and places him among those who have debased the novel as an art form.

2. *Periodicals*

ALDRIDGE, JOHN W. "Highbrow Authors and Middlebrow Books," *Playboy*, XI (April, 1964), 119, 166-74. Defines the current status of the "middlebrow novel," setting forth O'Hara and Styron as representative. Completely hostile to O'Hara.

"As 'From the Terrace' Goes to Press: Appointment with O'Hara," *Publisher's Weekly*, CLXXIV (Nov. 3, 1958), 22-23. Account of an interview with O'Hara, including some pertinent biographical data.

AUCHINLOSS, LOUIS. "Marquand and O'Hara: the Novel of Manners," *Nation*, CXCI (Nov. 19, 1960), 386-88. Asserts that O'Hara's is fundamentally a social novelist whose characters' destinies derive largely from their class position.

BADER, ARNO L. "The Structure of the Modern Short Story," *College English*, VII (Nov., 1945), 90-92. Advances a brief analysis of one of O'Hara's stories to illustrate that the modern story has a definite structure and narrative element.

BIER, JESSE. "O'Hara's *Appointment in Samarra:* His First and Only Real Novel," *College English,* XXV (Nov., 1963), 135-41. Offers sharp insights into O'Hara's first novel, stressing its use of military imagery to convey social conflict.

BISHOP, JOHN PEALE. "The Missing All," *Virginia Quarterly Review,* XIII (Jan., 1937), 106-21. This estimate of O'Hara as a post-Jazz Age disciple of Hemingway and Fitzgerald influenced the course of much later criticism. Concludes that O'Hara has skill but lacks warmth.

CERF, BENNETT. "Portrait of a Pro," *Saturday Review,* XXXVIII (June 11, 1955), 5-7. Illuminates some aspects of the writer's personality.

GARY, BEVERLY. "A Post Portrait: John O'Hara," New York *Post,* May 18-22, 24, 1959 (six installments). Of little value as literary criticism, but one of the most complete biographical accounts of O'Hara to date.

GIBBS, WOLCOTT. "Watch Out for Mr. O'Hara," *Saturday Review of Literature,* XVII (Feb. 19, 1938), 10-12. A subjective, humorous, but informative biographical sketch.

HUTCHENS, JOHN K. "John O'Hara From Pottsville, Pa.," New York *Herald Tribune Books* (Dec. 4, 1955), 2. Report of an interview, including noteworthy biographical detail.

"John O'Hara at 58: A Rage to Write," *Newsweek,* LXI (June 3, 1963), 54-57. A combination of biography and criticism; generally views O'Hara's career with favor.

KEATING, JACK. "John O'Hara's World of Yale, Society, and Sex," *Cosmopolitan,* CXLIX (Sept., 1960), 59-63. Contains some pertinent biographical material and a number of interesting comments by O'Hara.

NICHOLS, LEWIS. "Talk with John O'Hara," New York *Times Book Review* (Nov. 27, 1955), 16. Summary of an interview with O'Hara stressing his use of Pennsylvania material in his later novels.

PODHORETZ, NORMAN. "Gibbsville and New Leeds: the America of John O'Hara and Mary McCarthy," *Commentary,* XXI (March, 1956), 269-73. Sympathetic, cogent analysis of O'Hara; focuses on his depiction of sexuality and social status.

PORTZ, JOHN. "John O'Hara Up to Now," *College English,* XVII (May, 1955), 493-99, 516. A consistently hostile although intelligent and serious evaluation of O'Hara; concludes that he failed to develop after his early promise.

REICHLEY, JAMES. "Pottsville's Still Republican," *New Republic,* CXXXV (Nov. 5, 1956), 13-15. Illuminating political and economic survey of the writer's birthplace.

SCHWARTZ, DELMORE. "Smile and Grin, Relax and Collapse," *Partisan Review*, XVII (March, 1950), 292-96. Discussion of the *"New Yorker* story" pertinent to O'Hara's work.

WEAVER, ROBERT. "Twilight Area of Fiction: The Novels of John O'Hara," *Queen's Quarterly*, LXVI (Summer, 1959), 320-25. Places O'Hara among writers whose work incorporates a strongly realistic treatment of social milieu.

WELLES, BENJAMIN. "John O'Hara and His Pal Joey," *New York Times* (Jan. 26, 1941), sec. ix, 3. Biographical sketch including observations about O'Hara's personality and special talents.

WILSON, EDMUND. "The Boys in the Back Room: James M. Cain and John O'Hara," *New Republic*, CIII (Nov. 11, 1940), 665-66. Another of the enormously influential early estimates which has continued to shape subsequent discussion of O'Hara's work. Sees O'Hara as deriving from Hemingway.

3. *Reviews*: A Representative Selection

Appointment in Samarra

CANBY, HENRY SEIDEL. "Mr. O'Hara and the Vulgar School," *Saturday Review of Literature*, XI (Aug. 18, 1934), 53, 55.

BLACKMUR, R. P. "A Morality of Pointlessness," *Nation*, CXXXIX (Aug. 22, 1934), 220-21.

QUENNELL, PETER. "New Novels," *New Statesman and Nation*, VIII n.s. (Dec. 29, 1934), 972.

The Doctor's Son and Other Stories

MARSH, FRED T. "The Doctor's Son and Other Stories," New York *Herald Tribune Books* (March 3, 1935), p. 17.

Butterfield 8

STEVENS, GEORGE. "Appointment in Park Ave.," *Saturday Review of Literature*, XII (Oct. 19, 1935), 14.

TRILLING, LIONEL. "Mr. O'Hara's Talent," *Nation*, CXLI (Nov. 6, 1935), 545.

COWLEY, MALCOLM. "Hemingway Mixed with Hearst," *New Republic*, LXXXV (Dec. 4, 1935), 108-09.

Hope of Heaven

KAZIN, ALFRED. "Smeared with Glitter," New York *Herald Tribune Books* (March 20, 1938), p. 2.

Files on Parade

PRATT, FLETCHER. "O'Hara's Short Stories," *Saturday Review of Literature*, XX (Sept. 23, 1939), 7.

RUGOFF, MILTON. "Tough, Tender, and Swift-Paced," New York *Herald Tribune Books* (Sept. 24, 1939), p. 3.

Selected Bibliography

Pal Joey

ROTHMAN, N. L. "Dear Pal John," *Saturday Review of Literature*, XXIII (Oct. 26, 1940), 14.

VAN GELDER, ROBERT. "O'Hara's Portrait of a Night-Club Singer," New York *Times Book Review* (Nov. 3, 1940), p. 4.

Pipe Night

TRILLING, LIONEL. "John O'Hara Observes Our Mores," New York *Times Book Review* (March 18, 1945), p. 1, 9. Reprinted as the introduction to *Selected Short Stories of John O'Hara*, New York: Modern Library, 1957.

FEARING, KENNETH. "Perfidies of Life His Concern," New York *Herald Tribune Books* (March 25, 1945), p. 2.

ROSENFELD, ISAAC. "Racket or Tragedy," *New Republic*, CXII (May 14, 1945), 681-82.

Here's O'Hara

ROBINSON, HENRY MORTON. "O'Hara in His Time," *Saturday Review*, XXIX (May 18, 1946), 9.

WATTS, RICHARD JR. "O'Hara in Omnibus," *New Republic*, CXII (May 27, 1946), 777-78.

Hellbox

WOODBURN, JOHN. "Tattooed Portraits," *Saturday Review*, XXX (Aug. 9, 1947), 10.

"Ugly Moments," *Time*, L (Aug. 11, 1947), 98-99.

SULLIVAN, RICHARD. "O'Hara Short Stories: Bright, Bitter, 'Moral,'" New York *Times Book Review* (Aug. 17, 1947), p. 5.

A Rage to Live

GILL, BRENDAN. "The O'Hara Report and the Wit of Miss McCarthy," *New Yorker*, XXV (Aug. 20, 1949), 64-65.

SPECTORSKY, A. C. "Portrait of a Woman," New York *Times Book Review* (Aug. 21, 1949), p. 4.

PICKREL, PAUL. "Outstanding Novels," *Yale Review*, XXXIX (Fall, 1949), 191-92.

The Farmer's Hotel

JANEWAY, ELIZABETH. "Violence in the O'Hara Country," New York *Times Book Review* (Nov. 11, 1951), p. 5.

COOKE, ALISTAIR. "O'Hara's Joyless, Wonderfully Observed Little World," New York *Herald Tribune Books* (Nov. 18, 1951), p. 5.

Sweet and Sour

WILLIAMSON, SAMUEL T. "The O'Hara Swath," New York *Times Book Review* (Oct. 17, 1954), p. 30.

ROGOW, LEE. "O'Hara's Vaudeville," *Saturday Review*, XXXVII (Nov., 1954), 14-15.

Ten North Frederick

DAVIS, ROBERT GORHAM. "O'Hara's World of Secret Lives," New York *Times Book Review* (Nov. 27, 1955), p. 1.

GARDINER, H. C. "Drained of Drama," *America*, XCIV (Dec. 10, 1955), 307-8.

MCKELWAY, ST. CLAIR. "And Nothing But the Truth," *New Yorker*, XXXI (Dec. 17, 1955), 162, 165-66.

FIEDLER, LESLIE. "An Old Pro at Work," *New Republic*, CXXXIV (Jan. 9, 1956), 16-17.

ALEXANDER, SIDNEY. "Another Visit to O'Haraville," *Reporter*, XIV (Jan. 26, 1956), 44-47.

A Family Party

KELLY, JAMES. "A Doctor's Business," *Saturday Review*, XXXIX (Aug. 18, 1956), 14.

From the Terrace

"Limited View," *Times Literary Supplement* (London), Oct. 23, 1959, p. 605.

MIZENER, ARTHUR. "Something Went Seriously Wrong," New York *Times Book Review* (Nov. 23, 1958), p. 1, 14.

HICKS, GRANVILLE. "The Problem of O'Hara," *Saturday Review*, XLI (Nov. 29, 1958), 14-15.

WAIN, JOHN. "Snowed Under," *New Yorker*, XXXIV (Jan. 10, 1959), 112-14.

Ourselves to Know

BOROFF, DAVID. "A Desperate Detour to Destruction," *Saturday Review*, XLIII (Feb. 27, 1960), 23, 29.

MOORE, HARRY T. "The Murderer Tells His Story," New York *Times Book Review* (Feb. 28, 1960), p. 5.

ADAMS, PHOEBE. "Lolita in Pa.," *Atlantic Monthly*, CCV (March, 1960), 120-21.

Sermons and Soda Water

HICKS, GRANVILLE. "The Shorter, Short Novels," *Saturday Review*, XLIII (Dec. 10, 1960), 18.

STEINER, GEORGE. "Winter of Discontent," *Yale Review*, L (Spring, 1961), 425-26.

Five Plays

"Irving Said No," *Time*, CXXVIII (Aug. 18, 1961), 72.

TAUBMAN, HOWARD. "A Novelist in the Wings," New York *Times Book Review* (Aug. 20, 1961), p. 4.

Selected Bibliography

Assembly

HICKS, GRANVILLE. "A Deep Look at the Surface," *Saturday Review*, XLIV (Nov. 25, 1961), 21.

BOROFF, DAVID. "Chapters of America," New York *Times Book Review* (Nov. 26, 1961), pp. 4-5, 44.

HOWE, IRVING. "The Flaw in O'Hara," *New Republic*, CXLV (Nov. 27, 1961), 16-17.

The Big Laugh

SPECTOR, ROBERT DONALD. "Life and Times of a Hollywood Cad," New York *Herald Tribune Books* (May 27, 1962), p. 8.

MARX, ARTHUR. "Heelprints on Hollywood and Vine," *Saturday Review*, XLV (July 7, 1962), 29.

The Cape Cod Lighter

GUTWILLIG, ROBERT. "From Tiny Details, the Big Truth," New York *Times Book Review* (Nov. 25, 1962), pp. 1, 16.

PEDEN, WILLIAM. " 'Vanity Fair' Updated," *Saturday Review*, XLVI (Jan. 5, 1963), 39.

Elizabeth Appleton

WARE, CADE. "A Faculty Wife Joins the O'Hara Gallery," New York *Herald Tribune Books* (June 2, 1963), p. 4.

BOROFF, DAVID. "A Rage to Relive," *Saturday Review*, XLVI (June 8, 1963), 29-30.

GEISMAR, MAXWELL. "Who's Afraid of the Professor's Wife," New York *Times Book Review* (June 9, 1963), p. 7.

The Hat on the Bed

KEELEY, EDMUND. "Only a Few Trips from His Small, Tidy Realm," New York *Herald Tribune Books* (Dec. 1, 1963), p. 8.

"Seasonal Treat," *Newsweek*, LX (Dec. 2, 1963), 104.

VIDAL, GORE. "Appointment with O'Hara," *New York Review of Books*, II (April 16, 1964), 5-7.

The Horse Knows the Way

HICKS, GRANVILLE. "So Long to the Short for a While," *Saturday Review*, XLVII (Nov. 28, 1964), 21.

KAUFFMAN, STANLEY. *New York Review of Books*, III (Dec. 17, 1964), 21.

Index

73132

81352
G799

DATE DUE

GAYLORD   PRINTED IN U.S A.

73132